W9-CPW-047

FATHERHOOD
AN OWNER'S MANUAL

For Fathers of Children From Birth To Age Five

By

DOUG SPANGLER

Katie Spangler, Editor and Art Director
Jay Flom, Illustrator
Victor Ichioka, Cover Designer

FABUS PUBLISHING: Richmond, California

Copyright © 1994 by Doug Spangler
Manufactured in the United States of America
First Edition

Library of Congress Catalog Card Number: 93-71807

Publisher's Cataloging in Publication
Spangler, Doug.
    Fatherhood : an owner's manual : for fathers of children
from birth to age five / by Doug Spangler.
    p. cm.
    Includes index.
    ISBN 0-9631827-5-7

    1. Fathers. 2. Father and child. 3. Child rearing. 4.
Parenting. I. Title.

HQ756.S63 1994   306.8'742
                                  QBI93-915

This book is dedicated to my wife, Katie, and our children, Brian and Jenni—who are eyewitnesses to my oft-unusual driving, yet who still love me. No greater earthly love can a man have!

TABLE OF CONTENTS

PART ONE

PART TWO

-------PART ONE-------

SECTION I

INTRODUCTION TO OWNERSHIP

Congratulations and welcome to the growing numbers of fathers throughout the world. This Section introduces you to what it means to be a full-time owner/operator of your new fatherhood.

ASSUMING OWNERSHIP

When you begin ownership, you receive two keys: purpose and quality. What you do with them affects your lifelong enjoyment of fatherhood.

CHAPTER 1

Assuming Ownership

Fatherhood is like a car. Perhaps you've seen some men treat it as they would a rental. They drive it occasionally, usually on weekends. Then they dispose of it at the first sign of trouble. Others get someone else to chauffeur them around, refusing to take any responsibility for their fatherhoods' operations. And there are fathers who believe they can live as they want, designating other drivers when they're in no shape to get behind the wheel. None of these men are *full owners*.

This Manual's purpose is to help you understand what it means to assume ownership and undertake full operation of your brand new fatherhood.

Perhaps you feel inexperienced or insecure in your knowledge. All men do when they're new to fatherhood. But through intentional hands-on driving, you'll soon gain fatherly skills and confidence. Your child will benefit socially, spiritually, emotionally, and intellectually. Your marriage will grow stronger. And you'll find greater enjoyment and fulfillment throughout your entire life. Fatherhood fully *owned* doesn't diminish you. It completes and enriches you. With these benefits waiting, it's time to proceed.

The Keys To Your Fatherhood

As you assume ownership of your fatherhood, you receive two keys: *purpose* and *quality*. What you do with these keys determines how you'll start your fatherhood.

1. **Your fatherhood's purpose.**

Ask yourself, "What is the goal of my fatherhood?" This is important because it gets you out of your "gut mode" and into your "thinking mode." How you answer has far-reaching implications for your entire life.

If you start your fatherhood without thinking about its purpose, you'll soon find yourself getting lost, driving aimlessly, or having accident after accident. This situation isn't healthy for you or for anyone around you.

In times past, the purpose of fathering a child was often to gain another family worker, create status within a community, or assure the continuation of property rights. Kings would literally kill for a male heir to carry on the family name or solidify their power. Less influential men had similar concerns but followed through with less desperate measures. In many cases, to become a father was to become a man. Fatherhood was almost a one-time symbolic event— siring a child was proof of virility.

Today, thankfully, men are defining fatherhood much differently. And how you define your fatherhood determines your purpose.

What is fatherhood? Is it a role? Is it certain emotions or behaviors? Is it limited to parenting and your home-life? Is it serious or superficial? Is it important for your wife as well as your child?

Real fatherhood is a set of relationships.

It is NOT a role. A role is predetermined, strictly limited behavior that communicates particular ideas. Actors play roles. Notice, they do not live them. They're given certain lines, emotions, and behavior to perform because they're playing a part in recreating a story. But it is not their own story. It's a kind of fantasy. Their actual identities, thoughts, and feelings are never seen.

In *real* fatherhood, you're not playing a role. You're not just following a conventional "father" scenario (like playing ball, taking pictures, putting up and collapsing equipment, running to the store for "emergency" items, taking the baby out in the stroller on Saturdays, etc.). *In real fatherhood, you're being yourself as you establish, nurture, and grow in new relationships.* And these new relationships reach into every aspect of your life: career, marriage, friendships, parenthood, religion, personal growth, and extended family.

2. Your fatherhood's quality.

It's not enough just to define fatherhood as a set of relationships. You must also ask, "What will be the *quality* of those fatherhood relationships?"

There are many ways to start working out answers to this question. Most men develop their fatherhood ideas by observing their own fathers. If they had terrific dads, they may try to imitate them. Some incorporate only what they appreciated about their fathers and ignore the rest. If their relationships with their dads were poor, they might decide to do or be the exact opposite. Those who grew up without a father in the home may look to other men who exemplify fatherly traits.

You can also arrive at your own fathering ideas—ways you want to relate as a dad but may not see others doing. Or perhaps talking over parenting goals with your wife will help you clarify ideas about the nature of your own fatherhood.

It's useful here to think in terms of a close friendship. What are the characteristics you appreciate in a friend? Is he or she caring, thoughtful, fun to be with, a good listener? Is he there when you need him? Does she spend time with you, and love you despite your flaws? Is there a sense of trust that allows both of you to relax and be yourselves?

Actually these characteristics are important for all your relationships—whether friendships, marriage, parenting, or even your relationship with yourself. It's the *supportive* aspect that builds an enduring, quality bond.

An excellent way to focus on the *quality* of your fatherhood is to ask yourself, "What kind of relationship do I want to have with my child 20 years from now?"

Your answer might be, "I'd like a relationship of *love*, *respect*, and *concern*. I'd want open communication and opportunities to share time together. I'd like my adult child to feel free to come to me for advice. I'd appreciate being able to discuss my concerns with him or her. And I'd like to enjoy friendly family gatherings and celebrations." You may have more specific ideas to add, but everyone would probably agree to these basic goals. They will shape the quality of your relationships and everything you do as a father during the next 20 years and beyond. *Starting now.*

••••

The rest of **PART ONE** describes ways to establish and enrich your new fatherhood relationships. You will learn about your fatherhood's engine and how its components work together to provide maximum power. Understanding the operation of your gears, accelerator, steering, and brakes will help you drive effectively down life's various roadways. It also includes the necessary maps, information about major road hazards, and safe driving tips you will need for a smoother journey.

PART TWO of this Manual is intended for use after you've gained experience operating your fatherhood. It shows you how to keep your fatherhood in top form through preventative maintenance and regular tune-ups. You will also find valuable resources to increase your ownership enjoyment: Troubleshooting Guide, Thumbnail Sketch Of Child Development, How To Select Good Childcare, Reference Book List, and Children's Literature List.

Good luck and happy fathering!

SECTION II

BEFORE YOU BEGIN OPERATING YOUR FATHERHOOD

Before you start your fatherhood, you should know how it gets its power. Without this understanding, you won't be able to enjoy ownership. This Section describes the essential components of your fatherhood's four-cylinder engine: *Cylinders*, *Spark Plug*, and *Fuel*.

CYLINDERS

Personal Growth, Priorities, Partnership, and Parenting are the four cylinders. Each is unique and vital to a strong fatherhood.

SPARK PLUG

A spark plug gives the consistent charge needed to keep your fatherhood's cylinders operating together. The top-rated spark plug is your intentional commitment to be an involved dad.

FUEL

Choosing the right fuel for your fatherhood's engine is important for maximum performance and smooth operation. The Supreme quality fuel is father-love. This is the new depth and maturity of love you experience as a husband and father.

CHAPTER 2

Personal Growth Cylinder

Remember the car you drove as a teenager? Maybe it wasn't the best or fastest on the road. But what counted most was what it meant. For you, it was a coming of age. It brought you to a new level of opportunity, responsibility, and skill in managing your life.

Likewise, your fatherhood takes you to another stage in life. Some men consciously or unconsciously refuse to move to this new level. They leave the bulk of parenting to their wives, relatives, daycare workers, or preschool teachers. However, those who do assume full ownership find that fatherhood gives them new strengths.

Importance of Personal Growth

Your *personal growth* at this stage provides a vital power-stroke to your fatherhood's engine in three ways.

1. **Self-knowledge.**

They say that you really don't know what you're made of until you're tested. Pregnancy, birth, and early parenting are truly testing times. The changes they create in your life challenge your values, career, patience, emotions, finances, will power, stereotypes, physical strength, and marriage commitment. One of the positive results of this testing is increased self-knowledge. You're able to learn more about yourself and how you respond to new experiences.

Observing your child from birth to age five will help you understand that there's a certain pattern to human growth. A stable period is followed by an unstable time of transition to a new stage. Stability in that stage precedes another period of transition, and so on. (See Appendix B, Thumbnail Sketch Of Child Development, for further explanation.) This realization gives you a new perspective on yourself and your own growth. You can understand your strengths, weaknesses, and susceptibilities both in times of stability and during transitions.

Also, throughout pregnancy, birth, and early parenting, you will experience practically every feeling you can imagine—joy, lust, fear, grief, guilt, pride, anger, relief, excitement, frustration, jealousy, anxiety, insecurity, inadequacy, disappointment, overwhelming love, etc. The range and intensity of your emotions can surprise and upset you. You may not have known you could experience such heights or depths. But you do. And you're still alive and functioning. You're at a new stage of self-understanding and maturity. You're a new man. You're a *father*.

2. Self-acceptance.

Understanding the reality and normalcy of your range of feelings is the first step toward self-acceptance. After all, they're a great part of what make up *you*. Rejecting these feelings means rejecting yourself. And no one can operate a positive, effective fatherhood if he's doing that.

Some feelings, if not recognized and dealt with, can cause new fathers to say and do destructive things. You may feel strong urges to act out your fear, anxiety, frustration, or a sense of inadequacy in ways you never have before. Acknowledging your various fatherly feelings to yourself will help you gain perspective on them. This new awareness can enable you to talk about them with your wife and friends. That is far better than expressing any negative feelings in abusive or semi-abusive behavior. And it's more constructive than burying them in work or other activities that separate you from your family.

In addition, you may now have different professional or personal needs as a father. The responsibility of caring for a child, a reevaluation of your career goals, and a renewed interest in your extended family bring these new needs to your attention. Again, accepting them rather than ignoring their reality will give you a new energy for responding.

3. Self-confidence.

One problem new fathers often mention is loneliness. In the beginning, you can easily feel the "odd man out." Your wife may become more emotionally centered on herself and her experiences with the baby, and less attentive to your couple-relationship. You must focus more on her physical needs both before and after the birth. And because your sexual relations change in style and frequency, you can feel inadequate and frustrated as a husband.

In addition, a lot of people ask about how the mother and baby are doing, but not about you. Friends, family, neighbors, even passers-by on the street may assume you can't or don't take care of your baby. So they leave you out of any conversations concerning child care. If you have no support group or you can't talk to your own father, you may feel very much alone. This seriously affects any self-confidence you have about being a parent.

Also, daily life as a new parent is a problem in itself. Chances are, you've never had to struggle before with colic, rashes, diapering, infant feeding, bathing babies, rectal thermometers, and chronic sleep deprivation. If this is your second child, your ability to manage is tested even more by responding to the needs of two children at the same time.

Yet, there's a positive side to all of this. In adjusting to and resolving these situations, you develop new personal and coping skills. Practice not only makes "perfect," it also creates fathering experience and confidence.

CHAPTER 3

Priorities Cylinder

Whether you know it or not, you conduct your life according to personal values. These are the essential ideas and ideals you live by. Most were unconsciously "absorbed" from family and friends as you grew up.

For example, you may graduate from high school and automatically look around for a wife because "that's the way things are done here." The community supports the value of marriage right after high school (or even college). And your behavior tends to follow that value, even if it might not suit your personal needs.

Likewise, you may have learned to value making money. This could mean spending years preparing for a career that will give you a high rate of pay. Or to achieve the same goal, you may work extra hard and put in overtime to get promoted to higher paid positions.

You might seek personal power. You may not value money as much as the power to direct, control, or dominate others. This would lead you into jobs or leisure activities where you could accomplish that goal.

Or perhaps being accepted is an important value. This could drive you to please others, to make people laugh, or to spend your money on fashionable clothes.

Look at the variety of behaviors you exhibit, the decisions you make, and the lifestyle you pursue. You will find that they're all based on specific values.

You can live without ever critically examining or prioritizing your values. Life becomes fairly simple that way. You coast along from adolescence into young adulthood and marriage, almost on the surface of things. But with the birth of a child, suddenly your whole life is turned upside down. Your marriage is different. There are new choices, time conflicts, money pressures, and responsibilities. There's a need for different values or new priorities in your present value scheme.

Parenthood is a *crisis*. It's said that the Chinese word for crisis contains two characters: one meaning "challenge," the other meaning "opportunity." Becoming a father creates new opportunities in life, but at the same time it challenges your old values. The shock is that you weren't expecting this. You may have heard your friends talk about their new fathering experiences. Yet very few of them discussed how the realities of caring for a child affected their values.

The impact of this crisis compels you to look at the way you live. "What is important now? What am I doing with my life? What will I do with this baby? How can I cope with the jolt to my marriage or the changes in my lifestyle? What will happen to the values we've developed as a couple up to this point?"

Setting New Priorities

Here are three steps to help you evaluate your priorities now that you're a father.

1. **Examine what's happening to you, your marriage, and your family.**

You can relate this new experience to other crises you have lived through successfully. For example, moving away from home (to get married, go to college, join the military, or find a full-time job) was a crisis. It presented you with new challenges. Looking back on the experience, you can now appreciate the opportunities for personal growth you found in those challenges.

You also probably experienced each past crisis as a major emotional upheaval. This was because the life you had structured, or which was structured for you, was changing. You grew beyond the familiar boundaries of your lifestyle. You moved past the comfort zone of the known into the anxieties and fears of the unknown.

New fatherhood can be a difficult time for any man. Some men ignore the questions it raises, and thus fail to deal with them. Some acknowledge the difficulties parenthood presents, yet refuse to relate to them. Others, however, use this opportunity to reevaluate their lives and come to a new understanding of themselves, their family, and their work.

2. Decide what values you want to live by.

The process starts when you examine the values that governed your behavior before fatherhood. This phase of evaluation is not something you can gloss over. It takes time. It requires looking back over your life—where you came from, what you've done, what your parents and home-life were like, what religious experiences you've had, and what decisions you've made that are affecting you now. Looking at the broad picture as objectively as you can will help you discover what your major values were.

The next phase is to examine each of these old values in relation to your new experiences as a father. For example, consider your marriage and ask yourself:

- How has my relationship with my wife changed since our baby's birth?
- How do I feel about it?
- What do I want our future relationship to be like?

This last question helps you clarify, redefine, or reaffirm the values you want to live by now that you have a child.

Repeat these questions for each major area of your life—home, career, hobbies, friendships, religion, extended family relationships, etc.

3. Determine your top priority.

As you work through this decision process, you will no doubt find that values which deepen *family relationships* keep appearing.

You can see this in ideas such as, "spend more time with my wife," "be involved with my child," "make job decisions that increase my family time," "look into work benefits that apply to my family," "start saving for a bigger or better place to live so the family will be more comfortable," etc.

Your changed family structure has altered your life, presenting different challenges and opportunities. And the growing *relationships* in your new family are what you value most now.

Family relationships become, then, your acknowledged top priority. This is a tremendously important step. Remember, your values precede and produce behavior. *And you simply cannot operate your fatherhood with maximum power and enjoyment unless you've made family relationships your highest priority.*

Impact of Family Relationships Priority

Choosing this priority has implications for three major areas of your life.

1. **Your marriage.**

Before children (B.C. for short), you and your wife developed a certain style of relating to each other. You made decisions about your home, time, careers, resources, vacations, and friends based on how they impacted your couple relationship.

But after children (A.C.), everything changed and continues to change. Now your decisions are based on a different kind of family unit. It's one in which you both must anticipate and meet a child's non-negotiable needs for nurture, affection, and constant care. Couple needs and career needs may come into conflict with new family needs, creating some difficult choices.

2. **Your parenting.**

Whether or not you've had previous children, your family relationships priority has implications for your present parenting efforts. It will guide everything you do for or with your child. This includes major decisions about career goals or childcare arrangements, as well as daily interactions.

As a result, your relationship becomes intentional. For example, instead of giving "knee jerk" responses, you may find yourself analyzing situations. "Will this activity or reaction help improve and deepen my nurturing relationship with my child?"

Without family relationships as a top priority, it's practically impossible to develop positive, long-term *parenting* relationships.

3. Your personal lifestyle.

By applying this priority to every aspect of your life, you'll identify areas of your personal lifestyle you may want to change.

For instance, there's your *career*. When you become a father, you may experience a change in motivation about your work or career path. You realize the need for steady employment and the importance of benefits, promotions, or increasing pay raises. After all, there are more bills now. In your case, there may also be a change from two incomes to one, at least for a while. Or you might decide against a workaholic career or lifestyle in order to spend more time with your family.

Consider your *friends*. Having a baby puts you into another circle of friends—those who have children, as opposed to those who don't. There's such a large gulf between the two that in many cases you'll begin to see less and less of your childless friends. Your current interests and concerns are more likely to center around child-related issues. Many of your childless friends find these boring or can't fully understand them. You'll tend to gravitate to friendships with other fathers just because of similar parenting experiences. This results in a major change in your social life and support network.

Your feelings about *extended family* may also shift. Expanding your nuclear family with the addition of children creates new connections with your extended family—those aunts, uncles, cousins, parents, in-laws, and grandparents you may have ignored for a while. Your new sense of family will cause you to rethink or perhaps reestablish these relationships.

Your *leisure activities* change. Because of your new fathering responsibilities, you'll find yourself reconsidering your free time. You may not want to exercise right after work. Instead, you may prefer an early morning jog while everyone's still asleep. You might postpone all that backpacking you used to do on vacations. Or you could eliminate a hobby that takes you away from your family. You'll discover other things you can do in your spare time that won't have a negative effect on family life.

Intentionality

This is just a brief list of how choosing the family relationships value as your highest priority could impact your life. The most important point to remember is that when you choose it, you must do so with *intention*, *commitment*, and *follow-through*.

It's not the same as making a New Year's resolution—when today's decisions are discarded in two weeks. This is truly a New Life resolution, one that's meant for all aspects of your life. Otherwise it's not really a priority.

CHAPTER 4

Partnership Cylinder

When a couple starts having children, they tend to ignore their own relationship. Because this can weaken your marriage, it's precisely what you don't want to do. *Your marital relationship is the foundation for your positive childrearing.* If your partnership is weak, then your parenting will suffer. If it's strong—and kept strong—you'll both enjoy much greater success as parents.

A solid marital relationship is crucial for several reasons. First, it means that *lines of communication are open.* Good communication is essential for effective parenting. If you can't talk to each other, life is going to get very difficult when you try to decide on a consistent way to handle your child's behavior. You must also discuss the scheduling or division of labor for family-related activities, such as chores, shopping, childcare, school meetings, vacations, family visits, doctor appointments, and religious services. Otherwise you'll soon discover the true meaning of chaos.

Second, this relationship *creates mutual respect and support.* Parenting can cause a lot of frustration and anxiety. By supporting each other through the strength of your marriage, you help each other cope more effectively with these negative feelings.

And third, it *allows each partner to grow.* After all, parenting is the art of helping children grow up to be fully-functioning adults.

While you're doing that, you can also encourage each other's growth as individuals.

Ways Your Marriage Can Weaken

There are two major realities in early parenting that can disrupt your marriage relationship.

1. Stress.

As mentioned, having a child is actually a crisis time for your marriage. During pregnancy, your wife's moods, body, and interests change. You find yourself having to adapt your relationship in ways you never before thought necessary. And after the birth, your relationship doesn't snap back to what it was. Neither does your wife's body. You may become jealous and envious of the attention your wife and child receive. You may miss the exclusive relationship you once had with your wife. You may feel trapped by your new responsibilities. In short, your whole marriage is changing. Basically, what you need to understand is that it's normal to feel stress at this time—both as an individual and as a couple.

Marriage and parenting aren't easy. In fact, life isn't easy. This is why your wedding vows said that you'd continue to love each other no matter what came your way: "For richer or for poorer, in sickness and health, etc." These vows are in the wedding ceremony to remind you that you really don't live "happily ever after." You may encounter stress, sickness, problems, and financial hardships, as well as relaxation, health, enjoyment, and security.

But through it all, your vows can remind you of your commitment and dedication to building a life together and growing in your love. Bad times don't necessarily get you off balance, because you're expecting them. Your vows warned you about them. And the highest ecstasy in your relationship is tempered by the understanding that this particular feeling, although it reoccurs, can't be continuously sustained. This realistic attitude toward marriage can help you maintain a more balanced view of pregnancy, birth, and early parenting. And it relieves your marriage of a lot of unnecessary stress. (See Chapter 10 for personal stress-reducing strategies.)

2. Sex-role Stereotypes.

With the birth of children, sex-role stereotypes tend to appear, even in strong marriage relationships.

B.C., chances are good that a couple could develop and maintain an egalitarian lifestyle. But A.C., traditional sex-roles automatically click in. These behaviors often appear because it's still believed, incorrectly, that parenting is primarily a woman's job. These expectations can be conscious, unconscious, or both. But they're very real.

Basically, traditional sex-role stereotypes dictate that certain behavior is appropriate for men while other behavior is correct only for women. These societal and family expectations arise in both a man's mind as well as a woman's. So there is often a kind of underlying agreement about them.

For example, a common stereotype decrees that men take care of the car, yard, finances, and outside maintenance of the house. Women take care of the children, cooking, social activities, and cleaning the inside of the house. Mothers handle all of the emotional and psychological nurturing. While fathers handle only the discipline and physical side of parenting (from carting baby equipment to playing horsey or tossing footballs).

Stereotypes can vary from culture to culture. But essentially what they do is construct artificial and unnecessary power boundaries around individuals and within relationships. They limit growth and shut off whole portions of men's and women's development. For example, if men aren't supposed to nurture, how can they express their fatherly feelings or develop intimate personal relationships? Or if women aren't supposed to look after financial or mechanical matters, how will they learn to care for themselves or others?

Stereotypes demean, belittle, and unduly confine people to the detriment of their relationships. Yet we still continue to follow them. Why? Because we don't examine them critically.

By questioning such stereotypes with your wife, you can both work to restructure your partnership into one that centers on *relationships* not roles. Doing this will get you beyond the seductive

power of stereotypes which draw you into their comfortably familiar "prisons."

Your first step is to examine the stereotypes you've learned or
gathered as you've grown up. Look at how your father parented you.
Look at how your mother parented you. What did either say or do
through the years that defined what a "boy" or a "man" is? In what
ways do you now find yourself doing or saying exactly the same
things?

Secondly, look at how your culture, religion, or ethnic group
would complete the following statements:

> A father is a man who:_____
>
> A mother is a woman who:_____
>
> The man is the family breadwinner because:_____
>
> The woman is more qualified to care for children
>   because:_____
>
> The reasons a man can't physically, mentally, or emo-
>   tionally care for an infant are:_____
>
> A man shouldn't cry because:_____
>
> A good marriage is when:_____
>
> A baby first bonds with its:_____
>
> The proper toys for a boy (or a girl) are:_____

You may think of others, but these questions will help you and
your wife come to a better understanding of your hidden stereotypes.

The third step is to ask yourself, "What do *I* want from my
present relationship?" This will allow you to see what your marital
relationship needs really are and how these can best be met. The flip
side of this, of course, is to understand how sex-role stereotypes
may be negatively affecting your marriage by denying those needs.

Importance of Communication

To get beyond the stress and sex-role stereotypes to a better
marriage *relationship*, the primary area you must concentrate on is
communication. Simply put, if you have minimal or only a superficial level of communication, you have no true marriage relationship.

Some wedded couples with children can live together and call it a marriage. But unless they are verbally sharing values, life goals, parenting concerns, and emotional intimacy, they don't have a strong *marital relationship*.

Having a baby greatly affects communication patterns. For example, most new parents tend to focus on the baby's needs and disregard each other's. They don't seek out ways to discuss what's been happening to them, how each other feels about it, and what future plans they may have. This situation is further aggravated by the fact that both people are anxious, sleep-deprived, sexually frustrated, and very busy with the new responsibilities of parenthood.

Despite all that's happening, this isn't the time to ignore your marital relationship. Granted, parenthood will dictate a changed lifestyle. But this need not prevent the two of you from continuing to grow together as a couple.

Basic communication becomes more important now, even if you have to *plan time for it*. And this very fact is what disturbs most couples: you've lost all spontaneity in life. You must plan ahead for everything—whether love-making, a conversation, or an uninterrupted meal.

Basic communication requires taking time to share concerns with one another, listen to each other's feelings, and give emotional support and encouragement. These are what lie at the heart of any meaningful relationship. But they are absolutely vital to a growing *marital* relationship.

At the core of this kind of communication is a striving to understand the other person. This is not just a superficial knowledge (such as favorite foods, music, and the like), but a deep personal understanding. It means appreciating the other person's growth, dreams, ideas, values, and emotional life. And what's interesting about working to understand another person is that you can't achieve it without sharing yourself. So it's a giving and receiving proposition.

Sharing our emotional lives is precisely where a lot of us men run into problems. Our upbringing emphasized that surface appearance counts more than anything else. Remember, "Clothes make the man" or "Get your game-face on"? Growing up, we considered it a weakness if we showed our emotions. And we didn't want to appear stupid, awkward, vulnerable, or out of control. So we haven't gained much experience or confidence in revealing our emotional depths. Thus when we're in situations that are emotionally intense, we may feel very unsure of ourselves.

It's OK to feel worried, concerned, fearful, anxious, upset, passionate, frustrated, or sympathetic. When you can acknowledge these feelings to yourself, you'll become increasingly comfortable communicating them. And what better person could you tell these to than your wife?

Also, as parents you'll experience new kinds of feelings. It's helpful if you can identify those feelings and share them with each other. This is the beginning of building a deeper level of emotional support in your relationship. Emotional vulnerability which was once seen as a weakness can instead become a source of new power and comfort in your fatherhood.

Understanding Each Other's Definitions

An excellent way for you and your wife to develop emotional support is to share important definitions with each other. It's the *first step* to truly understanding and communicating your individual and mutual needs.

Take your concept of love, for example. What is your definition of "love"? What are its elements? How does it feel? How is it lived out? How do you know when you are loved?

How you define love determines how you give and receive it. But if you ask your wife what love is, chances are she *defines* it differently. *This is where communication problems start.*

Imagine two people in a card game—a game called LOVE. The object of the game is to give and receive LOVE cards. You define LOVE as giving and receiving club cards. Your wife, however, believes that giving and receiving diamond cards means LOVE.

So you begin the game by giving your wife a club card or two. She looks at them and says to herself, "These are nice looking, but they're not LOVE. True LOVE cards are diamond cards. Why isn't he playing this game right? Doesn't he know it's the game of LOVE? He's supposed to give me LOVE cards. That's the object. Oh well, perhaps next time. If I give him some correct LOVE cards, maybe he'll get the hint."

With that, your wife gives you two diamond cards. You examine the cards, and observe them to be very nice ones. But they're not LOVE cards. You say to yourself, "Hey, I just gave LOVE to her and look what she gives me—something else! Doesn't she know that this is the game of LOVE? We're supposed to be giving each other LOVE cards. Why doesn't she do it? What's wrong with her? I don't understand her. She doesn't understand me!"

This goes on for a while until you are both angry, disappointed, or get up the nerve to ask why the other doesn't give any LOVE. The fact is that the two of you define "giving and receiving LOVE" differently. You're playing with different interpretations.

After you've heard and discussed each other's definitions, you restart the game.

By now you're sitting there with a few diamond cards stacked up, because your wife has been giving them to you and you didn't know what to do with them. You say to yourself, "I really do LOVE her. I want to express that LOVE. But I want to show it in a way that she truly understands. She's just told me that she interprets the act of giving and receiving diamond cards as LOVE. I don't interpret it this way. But if she does, I'll try it."

You then give her a diamond card, not necessarily feeling that you're doing a loving act, but intellectually knowing it. She is very pleased to receive the diamond card and gives you one of her club cards as an expression of her LOVE.

Both of you have found new ways to define and *communicate* LOVE. After a while, you each feel comfortable using them. You've discovered the true object of the game of LOVE and both of you have won. *In the game of LOVE, no one wins unless both win.*

A Constructive Communication Method

True marital communication occurs when you both understand how *the other* sees and approaches life. And, of course, this includes how one loves. Through this kind of mutual understanding, a new relationship emerges. It's one with deep roots and the strength to endure.

It is not only important to discuss love, but also to define sex, marriage, husband, wife, father, mother, child, boy, girl, son, daughter, job, breadwinner, career path, housework, mutual respect, communication, and similar basic concepts.

In order to understand each other's various definitions, you need to use a different style of communication than the ordinary day-to-day kind. You must mutually commit to this process:

1. Listen, without interrupting, to your spouse's thoughts and feelings.
2. Repeat in your own words what you believe she's saying.

3. Have her acknowledge whether or not you've grasped her meaning. If not, keep trying steps 1 and 2 until she's satisfied that you understand her.

4. Explain your own ideas or feelings (which is step 1 for her).

Here's an example of how this might sound:

She: I always thought a husband would do his fair share of the housework.

He: You believe a husband should do, say, 50% of the household chores.

She: Well, yes. Although I never thought of putting an actual percentage to it. But, yes, I think it should be split evenly. After all, we both live here.

He: A husband and wife should split the household chores 50-50.

She: Yes.

He: When I grew up, my mother did all the housework. So I guess I just sort of assumed my wife would too.

She: You believe that a wife should do all the housework.

He: Yes.

At this point you've arrived at each other's *present* definitions. This is where you want to be. Now you can proceed to discuss your actual needs, work demands, time schedules, etc. Then you can *negotiate* any specific problem areas. (See how in the various tune-up chapters of Section V.)

This communication method will help both of you understand each other and resolve any real differences you may have. It will help you give the emotional support to one another that is so necessary during the first few years of parenting. It will also allow you opportunities to express your true needs and feelings as they arise—instead of ignoring or repressing them, hoping they'll go away.

CHAPTER 5

Parenting Cylinder

Parenting is a unique relationship that brings with it awesome and lifelong responsibilities.

Many men mistakenly see only the obligation side of parenthood, looking on it as a kind of "job." But the responsibility of raising children to be well-adjusted adults is undertaken in the context of a special relationship. And the quality of this relationship is far more important than the "job" of parenting. So your primary goal should be to develop a solid *parenting relationship* with your child.

Your own childraising ideas can be a major stumbling block to this kind of relationship. As you grew up, you collected information and impressions about parenting. They came from a variety of sources: what your parents did or didn't do, what you thought should be done, what you read about or saw others doing, your experiences caring for children, and so on. Currently, you may be influenced by what your culture says about parenting or what your extended family advises.

Ideas about childraising come from so many different sources that there's no logical relationship among them. It can become quite confusing. Consequently, as a beginning father, you tend to use a variety of parenting styles all at the same time. These styles are what you should examine.

For example, if you firmly believe both that a child "shouldn't tattle" and that she should bring her problems to you, you have some conflicting concepts. You may think boys shouldn't cry; yet you know men raised with that idea have difficulty expressing their emotions and developing intimacy. Or what happens when you try to instill the value of nonviolence, but you also believe children should learn to defend themselves?

Now is the time to consider the different ideas you've collected over the years. What kind of guides are they for *your* fatherhood? To what degree do they limit you and your child by encouraging sex-role stereotypes or discouraging open communication?

In order to develop an effective fatherhood, each man must get beyond these parenting styles and stereotypes. What really matters is your *relationship* with your child. A good father-child relationship does not result from "acting" like a strong father. It's the other way around. *You become a powerful father by first building a positive parenting relationship.*

As mentioned, this is to be a *parenting* relationship. Men have different interpretations about the parenting side of this. Some see it as justifying or requiring an over-under relationship—one where parental power is primary. This creates a home environment in which the parent wants ultimate control over a child. "Do it because I say so." Others may see parenting as an inconvenience, or something to be endured. This produces more of a hands-off approach. "The kids will raise themselves."

Neither one of these extremes builds any kind of meaningful, *positive relationship* between father and child. In fact, both approaches can unwittingly pass along dysfunctional traits. Perhaps you've been on the child side of one of these relationships and know the pain or emptiness of this experience.

The friendship model is recommended for building a satisfying parenting relationship. The types of things you do as you develop a close friendship are the same kinds of things to do with your child. This is not to say that your basic relationship with your child is just a friendship. It means that, although you have a parenting relationship, it's a friendly one.

How do you build a relationship with a friend? There are several important factors. You spend time together. You get to know each other personally. You recognize and appreciate each other's good qualities. You treat your friend as a separate individual, not an extension of yourself. You go through rough times and good times together, and develop a history. You are available to support and encourage each other. You get into conversations about important things. You communicate honestly. You respect each other's differences. And so on.

This is how you build a strong friendship. And knowing that you have developed this kind of relationship with friends before, you can feel confident about building one with your child in very similar ways. It's really not as difficult or as mysterious as it may seem at first.

Here's What It Takes

Building a positive father-child relationship will involve the following six features.

1. Participation.

It makes sense that in order to have a meaningful relationship, you have to be involved in each other's lives. At first, however, you may feel like you're the one doing it all. And this is true to an extent. But many studies have found that even an infant can respond to you and will actively participate, although in a very limited way, in a relationship. The older your child gets, the more she can become involved in your life. And the more she will understand you as a person. The key is to find the level of interaction she is capable of and work with that.

There are two aspects to participation in the life of your child: *understanding her* and *building your relationship*.

Getting to know your child is a key factor. One of the surprises you first encounter in parenting is that each child is born with his own temperament. This is a basic building block of personality. Observing your children over time, you will discover consistent differences between them that were evident at birth. (These temperamental differences are discussed in more detail in Chapter 11, Road Maps.)

However, just as there are differences among all children, there are also basic *similarities*. Each child is born with the same emotional and psychological needs. These never change as the years go by.

- Your child needs *affection*—and plenty of it. This includes physical (hugging, holding, kissing, comforting) as well as emotional (listening, encouraging, genuine interest). A child needs more than to be loved; he needs to believe he's loved.
- Your child is born with the need for *affirmation*. She should be recognized and affirmed from the beginning as a person who is important and unique.
- Your child needs *respect*. Your child's play, work, skills, body, ideas, concerns, and feelings deserve understanding and appreciation. They are as important as yours.
- And your child needs *security*. Much of parenting involves providing for the physical safety and emotional security of your child. This includes establishing and keeping limits on her behavior to help her feel she's protected and cared for.

Understanding both your child's uniqueness and her basic needs will allow you many opportunities for meaningful participation in her life. It provides the rationale for everything you do as a parent.

Building your relationship with your child is the other aspect of participation.

You may hear a lot about bonding with your infant. And you may have been led to believe that father-child bonding is a single critical event which happens right after birth. There's no doubt that you should begin your relationship as soon as possible. In fact, newborns can and do respond to your loving touch and care. But bonding only starts there. Building a relationship with your child is not the result of one occasion. It's accomplished over time, beginning with your first meeting. In fact, you never really stop bonding through all your parenting years.

Here's what it takes to begin a relationship and keep it growing.

- *Be fully present.* Did you ever talk to someone when you knew his mind was elsewhere? He wasn't "fully present" with you. It's difficult to relate to someone like that, let alone trust that he cares about you.
- *Be aware.* Being aware of the other person means knowing what's going on in her life. What have the past day, week, or month been like? Have there been any joys, failures, disappointments, or achievements? What are her emotions? Can you put her present situation into a wider personal context?
- *Communicate.* In any relationship there has to be real communication—the ability to give and receive understandable messages in order to express feelings, thoughts, or needs. Without regular communication, there can be no deepening attachment. Without the sharing of your personal selves, there is no relationship.
- *Maintain eye contact.* When you're talking together (even with an infant), eye contact is essential. This also means getting to the same eye level. Lift your child up to your level, or kneel down at his. This contact is one of two vital links between you.
- *Maintain physical touch.* The other vital link is touch. A loving touch conveys that you are fully present and aware of the other person. Touch gives you a chance to physically reinforce joy, love, sympathy, comfort, and encouragement.
- *Be consistent.* Positive, growing relationships are consistent. There are many opportunities for communication and interaction. And each person can trust that there is a sense of love and constancy underlying their time together.

You will find that being present, aware, and consistent are important for relating to your child at any age. However, you must vary communication, eye contact, and touch according to your child's development. For example, when he's an *infant*, your physical touch is constant due to holding him. Eye contact between you will last only a few moments at a time. And his verbal communication will be limited to sounds, laughter, and crying. When your child is a mobile *toddler*, physical touch is important but not constant. Eye contact can last longer. And your child may understand most of your words but not be able to reciprocate with conversation. As your child grows through the *preschool* years, physical touch again varies, eye contact lengthens, and verbal communication increases in complexity.

This kind of growing relationship requires that you take *responsibility* for participation in your child's life. You have just as much responsibility to nurture your child as your wife does—no less. Caring for children does not lie entirely nor even primarily with the mother. *It's a parental responsibility.* And you are a parent. Get involved and learn all the skills necessary for the complete care of your child (including bathing, diapering, feeding, comforting, washing clothes, choosing toys, reading books, visiting the doctor, administering medicine, making decisions about childcare, and planning ahead for your child's needs). When you do this from the beginning, you'll discover why responsible fathers report a deeper level of joy, pleasure, and confidence in fatherhood.

You are your child's father. As such, you must understand that you are extremely valuable and important to him throughout his life. In fact, your child has a basic "father hunger" or need for your loving relationship. Only you can fill it. No one can take your place. *Ever.* Your active participation in nurturing him from the beginning of his life is what full fatherhood ownership is all about.

2. Power.

All human relationships have an element of power in them. This includes any father-child relationship.

Whether you know it or not, you gain a high degree of power over your child just by being a parent. You have the opportunity to help another human being grow. This means you must exercise whatever skills you have (or can develop) to teach, nurture, and persuade your child toward meaningful adulthood. Because of this, your parental power becomes extremely important in the relationship you build with your child.

If you look around, you'll see men who don't realize this. They let machismo or competitiveness pollute their parental power. Some fathers misuse it by insisting that their home-life and parenting serve their personal needs. While others try to increase their power by dominating or abusing their wives and children.

The question to ask yourself is, "How am I going to use my power?" You can use it to serve selfish needs or to build your relationship with your child. Which of these meets your family relationships priority?

If you choose the latter, then your father power will be a positive support for your child—guiding, nurturing, and encouraging his growth. You can use it to create an atmosphere in your home where each person is important and valued. This is the way to achieve the kind of positive influence over your child that you seek.

3. Patience.

Children can seem to grow very slowly. Most of us men want them to develop quickly. We'd like our children to dress themselves, use the bathroom properly, and eat without making a mess all before they're a year old. We're eager to share some of the pleasures we remember from our own childhood. We want the years to go quickly so we can get out in the yard to pass the ball around.

But as we all find out, it doesn't happen like that. Many opportunities come along in parenthood to help us develop patience. Teething, spilled juice, house clutter, discipline problems, increased noise level, untimely interruptions, incessant demands for attention, and sickness coming at the "wrong" time for our work or vacation schedules are just a few.

As much as we'd sometimes like to, we really can't rush the social, physical, spiritual, emotional, or intellectual growth of our children. Men who try eventually find that this strategy backfires. Patience with children and their development during the first five years is very important. So is patience with yourself as you grow and improve as a father.

4. Planning.

Fatherhood requires planning skills. Spontaneity is no longer a part of your lifestyle. With a small child you're just not able to go anywhere on the spur of the moment.

Is the diaper bag well-stocked? What about toys and baby equipment? Is where you're going safe for small children? Is this a good time to take your child out or will it interrupt her nap? And what about her feeding schedule? You need to consider these questions and others like them before you head out the door. Then you must carefully follow through on the answers. Planning ahead eventually becomes second nature for even the simplest activities.

On the other hand, you can't make some plans too far ahead of time. For example, you may want to arrange parenting responsibilities for your own convenience, "I don't have time to take you to the park now, but let's agree to go the third Saturday of next month." This just doesn't work when fathering young children. They have very little, if any, sense of time. Infants know nothing more than the present moment. And preschoolers have trouble seeing beyond this weekend. Consequently, adult-centered plans frequently must be changed, postponed, or eliminated to accommodate the immediacy of children's needs.

5. **Physical effort.**

Your child's first five years of life are a very physical parenting time. Initially, you must do everything for the child—bathing, dressing, rocking, diapering, carrying, etc. Add to this all the baby equipment you take with you whenever you go somewhere (diaper bag, playpen, stroller, high chair, and the like).

As your child gets older, he becomes more mobile, and so do you. Much of your time is spent actively playing, physically redirecting him from mischief or danger, holding him close when he's "out of self-control," etc. This means that during the early parenting years you must make the physical effort of getting off the couch. You cannot nurture or discipline merely by verbal commands.

6. Perspective.

Like all things in life, fatherhood has its ups and downs. What's needed is perspective.

It's so easy in the early years of parenting to focus only on the day-to-day activities—sometimes even your child's hour-to-hour needs. When you do, you tend to lose touch with the long-term nature of your father-child relationship.

"Stepping back" every so often to see the overall picture helps keep you from exaggerating temporary difficulties out of proportion. You can begin to build a positive parenting perspective. This will enable you to relax more on a daily basis. It can also help you enjoy a friendlier father-child relationship. And you'll find yourself personally growing in a deeper appreciation of fatherhood—not playing the *role* of father, but being a *real* father.

••••

Your fatherhood's engine operates best when it's running on all four cylinders: Personal Growth, Priorities, Partnership, and Parenting. They're made to work in harmony and balance. If any one is weak or absent, they are all affected and your fatherhood loses precious power.

CHAPTER 6

Spark Plug

Another important factor you must consider before you start your fatherhood's engine is the quality of your spark plug. You can have well-built cylinders operating in synchronization, but without a good spark plug you'll spurt and putt along. As a result, you won't get the operational satisfaction you want or expect.

The spark plug with the Manufacturer's highest recommendation is *your intentional commitment to be an involved father*.

Intentional means fathering is something you've thought about and value. You are determined to use your reason to guide you. You won't blindly follow instinct or gut feelings. Your basic mode of parenting is pro-active, not reactive. You observe your child's temperament and needs, learn what to expect at different stages of growth, make family relationships a priority, and parent in ways that build on all these.

Commitment means that you are dedicating yourself to fatherhood along the lines of your wedding vows: "For better or worse, for richer or poorer, in sickness and in health, from this day forward as long as I live." It means fathering at 3 a.m. as well as 7 p.m. It means taking responsibility for child care when your child is frustrating and obstinate as well as when she's cuddly and cheerful. It's cleaning her dirty diapers as well as her dirty hands. It means turning off the TV and reading to her during the day as well as at bedtime. And it's taking trips with her to the doctor as well as to the park.

Involved means that your aim is to establish and maintain a positive, growing relationship—one that's multi-faceted and not bound by stereotypes. You will seek out ways to understand your child as an individual. You will encourage him to get to know you personally. You will be available to him through tears, fears, laughter, challenges, or misbehavior. In short, you will fully participate in nurturing and caring for him. To help you get off to a good start, ask your employer about the benefits of the Family And Medical Leave Act. They could give you at least 12 weeks of unpaid leave for your child's birth or adoption.

Using this kind of spark plug is crucial for a powerful fatherhood engine. It provides the proper charge to start and keep your cylinders moving in harmony.

You can use inferior spark plugs, such as "your occasional desire to do something with your child," "your reluctant agreement to feed the baby, but your refusal to change diapers," or even "your decision to let your wife handle the babies and then help out when your children are older—much older." These spark plugs, and others like them, can indeed start your cylinders moving. But they have inconsistent fire power, a weak charge, and an inability to withstand even minimal wear-and-tear.

This is not what you want. You want your engine's cylinders to work at peak performance and give steady power. So consider carefully the quality of your spark plug. And use only what the Manufacturer recommends.

CHAPTER 7

Fuel

Your fuel keeps all the elements of your engine working with maximum performance.

The kind you use is basically your choice. You can pick poor quality fuel which will clog up your plugs and cause damaging deposits in your cylinders. Or if you want to keep your engine running smoothly, you can choose Supreme.

Supreme fuel is your *father-love*. This is the new depth and maturity of love you feel for your wife because of your shared experiences during pregnancy and childbirth. And it's the love for your baby which enables you to care for him daily with tenderness, understanding, and unselfishness.

Remember your feelings when your child was born? Many men report this as an unexpected religious experience. They feel in touch with and part of a universal creative force, or the Creator Father God. The miracle of birth can indeed take your thoughts and emotions to a spiritual level that your previous life experiences were unable to do. Most fathers describe this as one of the greatest moments of their lives.

It triggers something in them that they never realized was there. It starts their *father-love*. This is the warm feeling you have when you think of your child as you work or commute, and your eagerness to see him when you arrive home. It's the excitement of watching your baby learn some new behavior or pass a developmental milestone like smiling, sitting, or walking. You find it in the pleasure of your child's spontaneous hugs and kisses. It's your concern that even when he misbehaves, you want him to be the best that he can.

The amazing thing is that you never run out of this fuel. Even though you may have used a lot of energy, your tank is always full. It's replenished automatically.

This seems contradictory. But you have experienced the same principle in other areas of life. For instance, in order to gain physical energy, you must first expend it in some sort of exercise. That's the way you build stamina. You don't achieve it by sitting on the couch. Or consider the familiar sayings: "In order to have a friend, be one," "To have love, you must give it away," and "It takes money to make money."

One reason this may be difficult to understand is that we're all used to thinking in terms of consumption and finite quantity. How can something that gets used be replenished without putting more back? But father-love is a *quality* of love—not a quantity. You will never run out if you keep the quality high by using it daily. The way it loses effectiveness and power is to keep it all to yourself or save it for specific situations. Then it's like a pond that has no outlet— it becomes stagnant and unable to sustain life.

In the past, and too often in the present, men have tried to show their love in ways other than by developing personal relationships. They work long hours to support their wives and children, thinking they're expressing their father-love most effectively through their paychecks. Or they constantly buy gifts, clothes, or classes for their children. Material goods become a substitute for their time and attention. Other fathers have good intentions of expressing their love personally—but put it off until later (when they've read the newspaper, after the lawn is mowed, after the next business trip or promotion, or when the baby is older and can interact more).

But *by themselves*, gifts, money, good intentions, achieving great honors, or working long hours on the job don't express your father-love to your children. Instead they express alienation and the inability to communicate or to develop a personal relationship.

The key to meaningful father-love is to personally show your love *first*. Don't wait around for others to say they care. Take the initiative daily to tell your wife and child(ren), "*I love you*." Also express it physically through warm hugs, kisses, active play, holding, and comforting. Spend time together as a family and one-on-one. Get to know each family member as a unique individual through anticipating and meeting his or her physical and emotional needs.

This Supreme grade of father-love fuels your engine with the quality staying power it requires.

••••

Understanding what powers your fatherhood is so very important that it cannot be overstated. Your fatherhood works because of the individual strengths of your cylinders, spark plug, and fuel—and the interrelation among them.

This Section has introduced you to the basics of your engine. With an understanding of personal growth, priorities, partnership, parenting, intentional commitment, involvement, and father-love, you're now ready to start driving. Section III will describe hands-on operation.

SECTION III

OPERATING YOUR FATHERHOOD

Important note to owners: if you haven't read **Section II, Before You Begin Operating Your Fatherhood**, do so now. Do not skip over it. That Section gives you a basic understanding of how your fatherhood's engine gets its power. This Section will describe four important elements in operating your fatherhood: *Gears, Accelerator, Steering,* and *Brakes.*

GEARS AND ACCELERATOR

Road conditions may vary on your journey. A successful fatherhood requires flexibility in speed and shifting. Your gears and accelerator provide those features.

STEERING

In order to negotiate your route and drive past any traffic problem, you'll need good steering skills and finesse.

BRAKES

Brakes are also an essential component of your fatherhood. They help you exercise the self-control you need to ensure the safety and security of all family members.

CHAPTER 8

Gears and Accelerator

Speed and its impact on your engine are very important factors in operating your fatherhood. This is why you must know about accelerating, decelerating, and shifting gears.

Without your accelerator and first gear, you wouldn't be able to pull away from the curb. Without utilizing different gears at varying speeds, you couldn't drive efficiently and safely in traffic. Nor would you be able to maneuver through the changes of terrain, weather, and road conditions on a long journey.

The accelerator and gears work together. Your accelerator varies your speed. Your gears help your engine run most efficiently at a particular speed to avoid burnout.

Unfortunately many men don't take advantage of these operational features. They maintain one speed, and use only one gear (usually the highest). Some are called workaholics. Others are labeled stubborn, insensitive, or non-communicative. They're used to charging through traffic regardless of the needs of those around them. When their first children are born, they experience the same difficulty in operating their fatherhoods as they do in operating their lives.

Fatherhood requires personal and interpersonal *flexibility*. Developing flexibility allows you to vary your speeds and downshift when necessary. These are important skills because slower speeds are crucial when small children are present.

As the owner of your fatherhood, you have total control over it. There's nothing automatic about your accelerator. You must determine the correct speed yourself. The gear shift is also manual. You must assess driving conditions and act accordingly. It is *you* who must operate your fatherhood intentionally and flexibly if you want to get anywhere.

Increasing Your Flexibility

Here's how to improve your skills in this area.

1. Recognize the need.

Early parenting demands daily decisions that impact your work, your marriage, and your family life. Because of this, you really can't live as independently as you have in the past. If you do, you will create unhappiness for yourself, as well as for those around you. Flexibility is a basic *need* for your fatherhood, beginning now.

2. Be prepared for changes.

A key ingredient in becoming more flexible is identifying your options. Find out from your employer in advance how you can take time off during the years your child is young. Can you flex your time? Do you have vacation, personal leave, family sick leave, or other time-related benefits? Find out the circumstances in which you can use these different leave categories.

Develop contingency plans with your wife for handling potential problems. What will you do if your daycare worker gets sick? Your baby must go to a doctor? Your child has an emergency medical problem during the day or night? Your car breaks down? Your Saturday night babysitter cancels at the last minute? Or an employer requires overtime? Talk to friends, neighbors, and family about their solutions to these kinds of problems. Call your local Childcare Referral Agency for information about resources in your community. Develop backup childcare plans. Then develop backup plans for those. The more you're prepared, the more options you'll have when unforeseen problems occur.

3. **Create personal flexibility.**

Look at your career, lifestyle, and time management methods. What aspects of your work, finances, or home-life cause you to be inflexible? Perhaps you have scheduled yourself too tightly. Or you're working longer hours than necessary. Maybe you've made too many personal or financial commitments, and you don't feel you can back out of them. Now is the time to reconsider those decisions and their implications for your fathering. Review your priorities. Make adjustments that will reduce unnecessary or self-made pressures and stress.

Try downshifting as you come home. Many men work all day with their adrenalin pumping, but don't go through a "cool down" period before arriving home. Then when they get there, they can't downshift fast enough for satisfying fatherhood relationships. This is reason enough to look into alternate means of commuting (public transportation, carpooling, etc.) which allow time for this transition.

The actual time you get home is also very important. Examine your situation carefully. Is your wife arriving earlier or later? Has she been caring for the baby all day? Whether he was home or in childcare, your child is probably tired and fussy. It may be that everyone gets back together in the evening with low energy, frazzled nerves, and cranky dispositions.

Work out with your wife what would help each of you at this time of day. For instance, you could take the child(ren) while your wife gets a short respite (or vice versa). You could develop a specific homecoming ritual (sit and rock with your child, all exercise together, share informal appetizers, etc.). The object is to shift more easily from the day's experiences into evening family life. This requires an *intentional* effort.

After you're home, look for specific opportunities throughout the evening to *care* for your child (bathing, changing diapers, feeding, burping, comforting distress, preparing for bed, etc.), as well as to play, talk, read, or just cuddle. If your child wants your attention, it's because she needs to be with you. Practice flexibility at these times. Put aside what you're doing to get involved with her. Of course, all of this applies to weekends as well.

Many new fathers wonder why their toddlers or preschoolers don't come to them for comfort. These fathers feel left out of the "parenting mainstream." Although children may exhibit specific parental preferences at different ages, one major reason could be that these men did not actively care for their children *from the beginning*. As a result, their children don't see them as a source of emotional and physical comfort. This is why your flexibility is so important right from the start.

Shifting gears and varying your speed are normal and expected parts of driving. Similarly, they are necessary for fathering. If you don't or can't slow down, you will miss your child's spectacular growth during her first five years. And you will deny yourself a personal relationship with her. You have already decided not to forego those. They're part of why you wanted to become a father in the first place. Remember?

CHAPTER 9

Steering

The primary way to steer your fatherhood successfully over the hills and around the sharp curves of early parenting is to use the *problem-solving method.*

Whether you run into an unexpected detour, get lost, or simply find yourself stuck in traffic—you have a problem. During early parenting, you're not alone with any problem. To one degree or another, your wife and child will share it. So it's important that problems are worked out for *the benefit of all involved.*

Typical fatherhood problems can stem from a variety of causes. A few are: losing sleep, changing jobs, deciding on daycare, making a major household move, handling your child's latest behavior, misunderstanding your wife's post-partum depression, regaining a satisfying sex life after childbirth, or sharing parental and household responsibilities with your wife.

Problem-Solving Method

Here's how to achieve a workable solution to any early parenting problem.

1. Identify the specific problem.

In parenting, what appears to be the problem frequently isn't. Usually something else is operating at a deeper level than the irritants that brought the problem to your attention. Since any two people see things differently, it will take some discussion with your wife to identify the real issue. This is one reason why you need straightforward communication.

For example, you may not feel like you're getting enough sex with your wife. This makes you increasingly grouchy and upset. Your irritability leads to arguments over your child's misbehavior. So it's possible to think that how to discipline is the problem in this case. In other situations it very well may be. But the real issue here is your dissatisfaction with your sexual relationship.

Or the problem could be just the opposite. You could be so angry at your wife's methods of discipline that you go to bed upset, uninterested in sex. The real issue isn't sexual incompatibility at this point, but a disagreement on how to handle your child.

If you both agree to discover the real source of any problem, you're on your way to successfully resolving the specific issue that needs addressing.

2. List a variety of solutions.

In most cases there is more than one way to solve a problem. Brainstorm as many solutions as you can. There is no need to evaluate them while they are being suggested. Evaluation at this stage can hamper creativity. Just list every possibility. Sometimes you may have to "sleep" on a problem to come up with a variety of good ideas.

If the problem is too little romance in your marriage, brainstorming might create a list like: 1) Get a regular babysitter and go out for an intimate dinner every other Friday night, 2) Have family or friends care for our child at their houses so we can spend a romantic evening at home, 3) Develop exchange sitting with friends, 4) Recreate romantic feelings with surprise gifts and messages, or 5) Put our child to bed earlier in the evening to create more couple-time.

3. Choose one.

Evaluate each proposed idea. Decide whether it would solve the problem. Then select the one you both like best. Or you may want to combine several ideas in developing a solution.

4. Commit yourselves to it.

This is a key element. You must mutually *commit* to take full advantage of this solution. You both want it to work.

5. Implement it.

Agree on when and how to start. Write it down. Then do it. Set a time limit for evaluating the solution. Depending on the problem, this evaluation could take place within a few days or up to several months after your decision.

6. Evaluate it.

At the prearranged time for evaluation, examine your solution. Did it achieve the goal? If not, how did it fall short? Does it need to be changed or improved in any way? Does it need to be scrapped altogether and a new solution chosen?

••••

Steering with this problem-solving method is a skill that will keep you safely on the road. Like every other aspect of operating your fatherhood, it gets easier with experience.

CHAPTER 10

Brakes

The purpose of your fatherhood's braking system is to slow you down or even, when necessary, to stop you in your tracks. Without adequate brakes, you couldn't possibly handle parenting's bumps, curves, hazards, or detours. You would soon crash, incurring pain and injury or expensive repair bills (not to mention possible lawsuits).

As noted, many of the experiences surrounding pregnancy, birth, and early parenting are very stressful. This is mainly because you must meet new responsibilities with diminished resources. For example, your energy is low due to lack of sleep. Your budget is strained by unexpected expenses. Less personal attention from your wife decreases your marital confidence. And then as your child grows, there's always a sense of being behind in responding to his physical and social development.

At the root of all this is a growing fear that you are losing control of your life. The need to feel back in control can produce some very negative results. For instance, if you have tried without success to soothe a crying baby, your frustration can lead to anger. And your anger can cause you to shake or hit your child. Or if your preschooler won't behave as you'd like, your anger could lead you to spank her into submission.

Indeed, a variety of frustrations occur in early parenting. If they continue or compound for any length of time, the stresses you feel become more and more difficult to manage. Often, then, just one more problematic situation causes a destructive loss of self-control.

This can happen to even the best of fathers. But it doesn't have to. The key to effective braking is learning how to handle frustrations as you go along. We can all sustain periodic problems. But when they build up, we need to employ different techniques. This is when we must use our brakes for intentional and functional self-control.

Strengthening Self-Control

Here are five steps to achieve this.

1. Develop deeper self-awareness.

The more you know about yourself, the more you will understand your skills, strengths, and, of course, your faults. The ability to identify your imperfections is essential for better self-control.

This need not be a negative experience. There's actually nothing wrong with having faults. After all, no one is perfect. But by understanding your weaknesses, you can become aware of what situations will be most stressful for you. You will recognize the circumstances under which you could lose self-control.

What are your faults? Has anyone complained of any? What would you secretly like to change about yourself? What would you improve? What characteristics would you like to develop? What were your New Year's resolutions for the past few years? Your answers to these questions will help you develop more self-awareness.

2. Tell your spouse.

This is the hard part. Admitting your faults to yourself is one thing. But it can be incredibly difficult to discuss them with someone else, even your spouse. Do it anyway. Often when you talk about your "soft spots," you're better able to pinpoint them and put them into perspective.

For example, there's a big difference between the broad assessment, "I'm no good in freeway traffic," and the specific insight, "It scares me when someone tailgates." With the latter, you can understand the actual source of any negative feelings, rather than operating with a vague sense of inadequacy.

Through this discussion, your spouse can help you find ways to strengthen or reestablish self-control. And you'll be able to help her with her own "soft spots."

3. Discover your specific emotions.

After a negative experience, you are most likely angry. But anger is deceiving because it doesn't reveal what you're really feeling.

Anger is a secondary emotion. It's actually caused by other feelings. A real or perceived threat to your self-worth or to your value system produces an emotional reaction. That reaction can be any one of several feelings, such as fear, guilt, shame, worry, fatigue, neglect, resentment, jealousy, frustration, anxiety, embarrassment, abandonment, indignation, rejection, etc. These feelings may then be expressed as anger.

So after you've acknowledged your anger, dig deeper to pinpoint the feeling that produced it. This will be extremely useful in helping you handle stressful situations. Once you've uncovered the real cause of your anger, it's a lot easier to deal with or control.

For example, suppose the emotion underlying your anger is fear about the effect of a childhood disease on your infant. Maybe more education about his treatment would reduce your strong reactions. If it's frustration because of not knowing how to soothe a fussy baby, help might lie in asking other dads what techniques they have found useful. If it's uncertainty about how to handle your child's misbehavior, you will find valuable information in child development books (see Appendix D, Reference Book List). If it's anxiety about leaving your baby for an evening, then you could ensure that your sitter is well-qualified through an interview and by checking references. If it's guilt about shouting at your wife "for no reason," then you might apologize to her and ask for forgiveness. If it's feeling neglected by your wife, you can discuss the matter to negotiate an acceptable solution.

Whatever feeling you have, you can do something constructive about it. This point cannot be overstated. There is hope for achieving self-control over any of the painful feelings you may experience as a new father. If you allow them to go unrecognized and build up, they can explode in fits of anger. But by applying brakes to them as you go along, you'll stay on the road to good fathering.

4. **Reduce stress.**

Many believe that stress is something that happens to you. In actuality, *stress is your reaction to specific situations.* How you view the events you encounter every day determines how much or how little stress you feel.

Did you ever wonder why one day you can be so upset by someone cutting you off on the freeway, and another time it doesn't bother you? That's because you see the same experience with a different frame of mind.

This is good news. It means that, although we can't always eliminate potentially stressful situations, we can do something about our reactions to them. And thus we can greatly reduce the amount of stress we feel.

The first step is to discover those situations or experiences in your life which prompt stress reactions. You may find there are particular things about your job, such as a bad commute, heavy workload, tight work schedule, frequent overtime, insensitive boss, job insecurity, no positive feedback, difficult fellow employees, etc. Or there may be situations at home, like bills, neighbors, arguments, car problems, home repairs, pet problems, child misbehavior, difficulties with family relationships, and so on. There may also be some personality traits within you that trigger stress reactions, such as impatience, perfectionism, no sense of humor, lack of flexibility, inability to relax, excessive frustration or anger, or the inability to limit outside commitments. These factors are different for all of us. That's why you will find some men really calm in situations that drive others to the point of losing self-control.

When you recognize what triggers your stress reactions, you're able to start doing something constructive about reducing those responses. Some men use drugs, alcohol, overwork, or infidelity to cope with stress. But these "solutions" or "attitude adjustments" don't really work. Whatever problems they were trying to avoid still remain. And new problems are invariably created by the supposed solutions.

What does work is to confront your problematic situations squarely and change your methods of dealing with them. First, you can use *short-term strategies* to reduce your immediate stress reactions:

- Take mini-breaks throughout your day.
- Do deep breathing exercises.
- Count to ten and think the situation over before you react. You may get a new perspective.
- Find someone to talk to about your feelings.
- Make a plan to organize your workload better.
- Keep perspective on day-to-day situations. Not every difficulty is a threat to you, your career, or your relationships.
- Forgive yourself for being human and making minor mistakes. Then move on.
- Do something nice for yourself every day.
- Get proper physical exercise.
- Talk to yourself positively, not negatively: "I can do it," "I'm OK as a person," "I deserve a break," etc.
- Hug your wife and child every day.
- Say "I love you" to your wife and child every day.
- Anticipate difficult situations and prepare for them.
- Learn as much as you can about child development to better understand your growing child.
- Laugh more.
- Start a hobby or make time for enjoyable recreation.
- Do a good turn daily (and try to do it anonymously).
- Communicate assertively, not aggressively.
- Control your weight and diet. Eat regular, relaxed meals.
- Develop new skills. Keep growing and improving. Do something different in your life periodically.
- Get things fixed as soon as possible. A stitch in time saves great aggravation later.
- Stop procrastinating on important things.

- Occasionally stop to smell a rose or pet a cat. Or, if you have allergies, listen to the birds sing, admire tree leaves, or watch a sunset.
- Hire a babysitter and take a break from parenting.
- Practice your personal flexibility daily. Don't sweat the small stuff.

And second, there are *long-term strategies* to consider:

- Set goals for your life and regularly review them. The feeling of going nowhere can pull you down faster than almost anything else.
- Find ways to work toward promotions or higher paying jobs that don't negatively affect your home-life.
- Work toward job security.
- Find adequate childcare, and make backup plans.
- Develop a Father Support Network (see Chapter 14, Preventative Maintenance).
- Improve your relationships with all your family members, especially your wife.
- Develop a vacation schedule that suits your lifestyle

but also helps you deal with accumulated stress more frequently than once a year.

- Go out with your wife as often as possible. Spend time talking, just like in the "old days."
- Develop and agree on household management plans with your wife.
- Buy products that will last (or that have a good repair record).
- Commit to performing regular fatherhood tune-ups (see Chapters 15 - 19).

These short- and long-term strategies (or others like them) will reduce the impact of stress-producing situations. You'll feel more in control of your life. This, in turn, will lessen your feelings of fear, frustration, anxiety, and so on. It will also strengthen your confidence about handling life's problems.

5. **If necessary, see a good counselor.**

If you find that the previous steps aren't really helping you manage your emotions, find a qualified professional to talk to. This can be an Employee Assistance Program Counselor at work; someone in your employer's Personnel or Medical Departments; a professional therapist; your personal doctor; a local parental stress organization; or your pastor, priest, or rabbi. Getting outside support and guidance in this way is not a sign of weakness or failure. It's a sign of strength. It says that you're serious about your fatherhood and want to keep it functioning as well as you possibly can.

Importance of Brakes

Your brakes are crucial to the effective operation of your fatherhood. If you slam them on suddenly or press too hard, you will probably find yourself in an uncontrollable skid. This is what you want to avoid. Brakes work better and last longer if you apply moderate pressure over a long distance, especially in stormy weather.

Proper braking techniques are very important for another reason. They will prevent you from losing control and abusing your child or wife.

Child abuse is not only physical. It can happen in one or more of the following ways:

- *Cruel Treatment.* The U.S. Constitution protects adults from "cruel and unusual punishment." Yet every day, some parents treat their children cruelly. This can include physical abuse, locking the child in a closet or other confined small space, withholding food as a punishment, demanding toilet training before a child is physically able, chaining or tying up a child to control him, or similar acts.

- *Emotional Abuse.* Some parental actions can be abusive to a child's feelings or emotional life. Examples are frequent teasing, manipulation, verbal harassment, constant family discord, apathy toward the child, negative communication patterns, belittling her experiences or feelings, and offering little if any physical affection or comfort. All parents may act in some of these ways at times. But it's when these are the child's usual experiences that they are abusive.

- *Mental Abuse.* This is playing power mind-games. It's when, for instance, you constantly yell, threaten, belittle, humiliate, or deliberately frighten a child in an attempt to control him.

- *Neglect.* For his own well-being, a child needs to be properly fed, clothed, supervised, and kept healthy. Refusing to fulfill these basic needs is neglect. Leaving a young child unattended is neglect. Not caring for a child's mental, physical and emotional health is neglect.

- *Physical Abuse.* This includes physical acts such as spanking, slapping, hitting, beating, shaking, pushing, punching, poking, pinching, whipping, throwing, biting, kicking, cutting, burning, yanking body parts, or torturing a child. It is any behavior that results in deliberately applied pain or physical injury to your child regardless of your intentions or the child's actions.

- *Sexual Abuse.* This includes inappropriate fondling or touching, attempts to titillate a child with various forms of pornography, sexual intercourse of any kind, coercing a child into sexual behavior, and the like.

Spousal abuse is very similar to this list. It may be cruel treatment, emotional abuse, mental abuse, neglect, physical abuse, or sexual abuse. Proper braking will ensure that you avoid them all.

NOTE: If you now have a problem or a potential problem with any of these behaviors (or someone has told you that you have one), please see a counselor immediately.

Negotiating Your Journey

Successfully operating your fatherhood means learning to shift gears, accelerate, steer, and brake. Without using these basic skills in harmony, you can't negotiate the variety of road conditions you will find on your journey. It requires taking other people's needs into consideration as well as your own power and smooth functioning. This is the purpose, after all, of being able to slow up, stop, change gears, or steer around problems. You cannot drive as if you're the only one on the road. If you do, your fatherhood will crash, seriously injuring your family and requiring costly repairs.

Since this is definitely not what you want, you must operate your fatherhood with the philosophy of *negotiation*. This means you strive for balance in meeting each family member's needs so that all can make it safely through the journey.

••••

Now that you understand what empowers your fatherhood and how it operates, you're able to get under way. In the next Section, you will learn about road maps that can keep you on course. You will discover the common road hazards. And you will review basic safe driving tips to make your journey smoother and more satisfying.

SECTION IV

INFORMATION FOR SAFER DRIVING

Safe driving is no accident. It requires choosing your route carefully, paying attention to road conditions, and intentionally improving your operating skills. The best way to safer driving is through obtaining accurate information and using it as you go along. The more informed you are, the more appropriate your decisions will be. And the happier your driving experience. This Section contains information on *Road Maps, Road Hazards,* and *Safe Driving Tips.*

ROAD MAPS

In order to plan your journey and keep on course, you need reliable road maps. In this chapter you will learn about two valuable sets of maps. Together they can provide the guidance you need to get where you want to go.

ROAD HAZARDS

Along the way, you will encounter road hazards. Any one of them can bring your fatherhood to a quick halt or cause serious damage. Here are ten of the most common hazards to watch for. Alert driving will give you the edge in avoiding them.

SAFE DRIVING TIPS

Every man needs to operate his fatherhood according to "rules of the road." Here are basic tips to help you in whatever traffic situation you find yourself.

CHAPTER 11

Road Maps

Too many men enter their fatherhoods and take off with little concept of where they're heading. This is a big mistake. Before you begin a long journey, you must consider the where, what, when, why, and how of the trip. Where am I going? What services will I need along the way? When do I start, take breaks, or arrive? Why do I want to choose a particular route? How am I going to do it?

In planning any unfamiliar trip, you need to consult *road maps.* The same is true for your fatherhood relationships. Because you're heading into new territory, obtaining good maps is a must. You will refer to them frequently along the way to keep yourself on course or plan alternate routes.

There are two important sets of road maps for your fatherhood.

Set One: How Your Child Grows

Many of us approach fatherhood with the mistaken ideas that all children are alike, that they grow in the same way, and that they have similar interests. Then we have children and find out nothing could be further from the truth.

Children are unique. They come in a variety of shapes and sizes, and with individual characteristics. If you and your wife have a second child, you'll soon see that he or she is different than your first. This experience amazes all of us. Because both children come from the same gene pool and home environment, we expect them to be very similar. Yet they aren't.

So, one of the first things to realize is that each child will develop according to his or her unique combination of *temperament, stages of growth, talents,* and *moods.* Admittedly, understanding each of these maps is one of the most difficult activities of your fatherhood. But the results are well worth your effort, and have a direct affect on the quality of your relationships.

1. **Temperament.**

Temperament refers to an innate personal style of behaving or reacting to life's various stimuli. Each of us is born with a certain basic temperament. We're consistent in maintaining this temperament throughout life. Sometimes we're able to soften its effects on our behavior. But we can never eliminate it.

Most children exhibit one of three distinct temperamental types.

The first of these is the *difficult* temperament. Fortunately, only about 10% of all children are in this category. A child who exhibits a difficult temperament is just that—difficult to parent. It's hard to establish a schedule or predict what may happen next. This child tends to react noisily and with intensity. He may exhibit violent tantrums. He will have irregular bowel functioning, daily routines, and sleeping patterns. And he's unable to adapt easily to new foods, people, or situations .

His temperament is not a threat to your authority nor does it show a lack of respect. And it's certainly not an indication of your failure as a parent. It's a factor of your child's uniqueness.

How, then, do you develop a positive fathering relationship with this type of child? Remember, your key relationship words are *love, respect,* and *concern.* Love your child despite any negative responses. Respect your child's temperament as a unique part of him, one which drives his difficult behavior. And show your concern by giving positive attention, affection, and acceptance to your child. Work *with* your child's temperament—not *against* it.

Through consistent and patient discipline, teach him how to manage his behavior and channel his energies in constructive ways.

Another type of temperament is the *slow-to-warm*. Experts say this characterizes about 15% of children. They are often mistakenly labeled "shy." Only most aren't. It just takes them a little longer to "warm up" to new toys, foods, people, teachers, preschools, animals, daycare situations, or any other stimuli.

This is the child who enters a play room slowly. He stands or sits apart from other children. He looks around and takes the whole scene in. Then he decides what area to go to first. And this is the child who prefers to wade slowly into the swimming pool after watching for a while. Perhaps he'll test it first with a finger or toe. Again, love, respect, and concern in your fathering will take this child's temperamental needs into account when making changes or beginning any new activity.

A third major category is the *easy* temperament. About 40% of all children are in this group. These children usually don't have strong, intense reactions to stimuli (like the difficult temperament) or take as long in making adjustments (like the slow-to-warm).

As a result, there's a broad range of behavior in this temperamental category. For example you may have a "jump right in" child. This one doesn't need to warm up to the swimming pool water or any other new activity, but just boldly plunges in. You may have a more passive, easy-going child. This is one who adapts quietly to schools, people, changes, or frustrations with very few problems. Or you may see any variation in between. Still, they're all in the same temperamental category.

From past observations you may suspect that not everyone exclusively exhibits one of these three temperaments. And you would be right. In fact, the figures above don't add up to 100% of the children. On one occasion or another, your child could behave in any of the three ways described or a combination of them. What you will see, however, is that over time most children favor one of these major temperamental patterns. *Which one is what you should try to discover about each child.*

You can find this out by closely watching and listening to your child over a long period of time, beginning at birth. If you do, you'll see that your child was born with a certain kind of temperament which remains consistent through the years. This very real part of your child's personality deserves your understanding. And knowing her temperament will help you choose ways to develop your relationship that are positive and constructive.

2. Stages of growth.

This is a map that most new fathers fail to consult. But it's vital if your goal is to build a positive relationship with your child through the years.

Looked at objectively, your child's rate of growth in the first five years is phenomenal. She goes from helplessness as a newborn (she can't even raise her head) to qualifying for kindergarten at about age five. In the few intervening years, she's learned to walk, talk, play, dress herself, feed herself, solve problems, use the bathroom, relate to people, and create ideas and objects. That's a lot of learning and growing.

But as you may know, it doesn't all happen at once. It's accomplished in small bits over time with many regressions. As your child acquires a new skill she must try it out, practice it, develop competence, and combine it in socially acceptable ways with all her other abilities.

If you haven't already observed it, you soon will. There's something within your child "pushing" him to grow physically, intellectually, emotionally, psychologically, and spiritually. There's a kind of "program" in his genes that keeps him developing on track. The specific *timing* of this "program" varies with each child, but the same *order* is there. And it has frequently been studied.

For example, children's baby teeth come in at about the same time and in a particular order. Babies crawl before walking, and walk at about the same age—give or take a few months. And who hasn't heard of the "terrible twos"? Somewhere between ages one and three each child goes through a period of emotional growth different than what she previously experienced. It occurs with each child, and is expressed with varying degrees of intensity depending on temperament. In fact the order of development is so consistent, you should look into it if your child skips any of the documented stages.

Each stage of development during the first five years moves your child into new territory. And whether it's a positive change or not, anything new for your child is unsettling. In fact, many new experiences are initially uncomfortable for you, too. Think about how you felt right after your last household move. It took you a while to get oriented to your new home, neighborhood, stores, commute routes, and support services. It temporarily disrupted your whole life.

Your child's experience is similar. He's growing into a different level of life—one filled with new skills, demands, pressures, frustrations, emotions, and opportunities. He may feel fear, anxiety, disorientation, and diminished self-confidence for a time until he's able to adjust to this developmental stage. And these emotions are magnified for your child by the newness of it all.

As a result, for the first five years of life it seems that your child is constantly moving from a stable period into an unstable transitional stage. This, in turn, leads to a new level of stability followed by yet another unsettling transition to the next stage. And so on.

What's important to understand is that these ups and downs are normal. They're part of growing up. Sometimes it may seem that your child is taking a step backward in his development. And this can be discouraging. But in the long run, he's in an upward growth process.

Unfortunately, we often interpret these natural developmental changes during transitions as rebellious, anti-social, or disrespectful of our authority. We may think something is wrong with our children, our parenting, or the family environment.

If we assume that our children are being purposely contrary or disrespectful, we'll soon find ourselves sidetracked from our primary goal. We need to understand that in those "difficult" times our children are experiencing real growing pains. With this perspective, we're better able to communicate our love, respect, and concern. For further information on understanding children's stages of growth and development, see Appendix B, Thumbnail Sketch Of Child Development.

3. **Talents.**

In addition to temperament and stages of growth, we can identify other behavior-shaping features in the first five years of a child's life. For example, each child has unique talents. These could be verbal, social, musical, athletic, artistic, mechanical, intellectual, etc. And just like temperament, your child seems to have them from birth.

The combinations can be quite surprising. You may have a child with musical and mechanical skills, one who's highly verbal and socially sensitive, or another who's both artistic and athletic. The possible combinations are without number. Many children exhibit more than a few talents.

You can discover your child's talents by giving her a variety of experiences and observing her inclinations. This provides you with very important information for charting a positive relationship.

4. **Moods.**

Moods are another significant feature of your child's makeup. Everyone, including your baby, has his ups and downs. Sometimes these last for days. Or each day can bring a range of different emotions.

Within a given day a child's mood can vary depending on what's happening. New, unexpected stimuli (a shopping trip) or a different schedule (a late nap) can quickly change his mood. You'll find that one day your child can tolerate these things, while the next he can't.

As your child grows older she becomes capable of an expanded mood range. She can experience stress, delight, rejection, depression, anxiety, and exhilaration all in the same day or within a few days.

What this shows us is that children have feelings. And their feelings are just as important to them as ours are to us even though they can't articulate them as well. It's easy for new parents to assume it doesn't matter what they do with a young child as long as he's properly fed, clothed, and cared for. This isn't so. Unless "cared for" includes taking into account the child's feelings.

It doesn't mean that we must cater to the child's every desire. It means that in mapping out any positive relationship, each person's feelings must be considered. The difficult part of this for fathers is that during the first five years, it's mostly a one-way street. Not until much later can your child fully appreciate your feelings and reciprocate your concern. But it's important for you to maintain this aspect of your relationship from the beginning.

Temperament, stages of growth, talents, moods—by observing, recognizing, and validating these, you're learning to see your growing child as an individual. Your greater knowledge of what motivates her behavior enables you to show your love, respect, and concern more effectively. This, in turn, leads to the deeper relationship you want. Using this set of road maps will help you anticipate and negotiate the hills, curves, and rough spots of your fatherhood's journey.

Set Two: Macro- and Micro-Parenting

This road map set shows two important ways of relating to your child and how they must be combined for effective fathering.

1. Macro-parenting.

Macro-parenting deals with your overall goals as a father. The way to discover these goals is to ask yourself, "What characteristics do I want my child to have as an adult?" List your ideas on paper.

You may want your child to be caring, friendly, honest, humorous, responsible, flexible, generous, creative, independent, dependable, intelligent, self-disciplined, emotionally mature, financially astute, capable of intimate relationships, etc.

If you analyze your list, you will see that it characterizes a fully functioning adult who's a positive contributor to society. These are personal attributes that will help your child enjoy a meaningful, happy adult life.

Take another look at the list. Your job as a parent is to help your child develop these characteristics. This list represents your macro-parenting goals.

So, when should you begin helping your child learn these important traits? At age 16? At age 10? At 5? Actually you can start at birth. Remember, the question was when do you *begin*, not when will your child exhibit the characteristic you're working on. The earlier you begin, the better. These traits are built slowly but surely throughout your child's life. Beginning today.

Teaching character traits is similar to teaching your child to walk. You do it by encouraging one small step at a time. You don't expect your toddler to run the hundred yard dash in 9.2 seconds. That kind of achievement takes years of Olympic-type training.

So it is with generosity or any other character trait. Generosity starts with something quite small—learning that a toy belongs to you. Later toddlers and preschoolers struggle with sharing what is theirs. But it's important for them to keep trying. Altruistic giving at an adult level is based on a child's eventually learning to share through having had many opportunities to master it.

Thus it's vital to see the connection between your end goal and what you're doing now. Just as you visualize your child running and dancing while you help her take those first shaky steps.

You don't blame your child for falling when she's learning to walk. In the same way you needn't criticize her for failing to master whatever personal skill you're trying to teach. What's necessary throughout your relationship are *reasonable goals, support, acceptance, encouragement,* and *a "let's try it again" attitude.*

If you reexamine the adult characteristics on your list, you'll see that each starts with one small step. Each develops slowly as your child grows. And each requires your constant encouragement and patient teaching.

2. Micro-parenting.

Micro-parenting is the other road map in this set. It can best be understood by looking at a specific issue. Let's consider discipline, one of the most difficult areas of parenting.

First, we need to gain a workable definition. As you know, individuals and entire cultures define discipline differently—from corporal punishment to reasoned discussions.

However, we must look at the root of the word to get at its true meaning. "Discipline" comes from the root word "disciple." And disciple refers to one who follows, one who learns. When there is a follower, there is also a leader or teacher. This person serves as a resource or guide for the disciple. So in parenthood, disciplining a child means the parent is *teaching* or guiding that child.

The question for parents is, "What should I be *teaching*?" The answer is your macro-parenting goals (your list of desired adult characteristics). Those traits should be the end products of your teaching, leading, or guiding. They're the goals of your discipline. And *how* you help your child learn them in a specific situation is your *micro-parenting.*

Micro-parenting means those things you do as a father on a daily basis. They *must always be connected to your macro-parenting* (the overall parenting goals you've developed). These two components really make up parenting. You can't develop effective, positive fathering without the interrelationship of both.

Unfortunately, too many men focus on the *micro*-parenting without regard for their *macro*-parenting. The result is that they relate to their children only on the basis of short-term goals and specific events. And too frequently those are concerned with expediency, such as keeping the children quiet or out of the way. This method of parenting doesn't really build a positive, enduring relationship.

Using the Two Together

Here's a way to connect your macro- and micro-parenting. When you're in a specific situation with your child and you feel he needs to learn something or change his behavior, stop. Before you say or do anything, tell yourself, "W.A.I.T., What Am I Teaching?" Quickly think about things. What is it your child needs to know? What macro-parenting goal needs reinforcing, even in some small way? You might see several things he must learn. If so, pick the one that is most important at the moment. Decide how best to teach it. Then proceed on that basis (micro-parenting). When you do, you'll not only discipline your child effectively but you'll deepen your relationship.

Combining macro- and micro-parenting in all situations, re-gardless of how minor they may seem, is very important for effective teaching. For example, assume your preschooler is being loud and persistently interrupts while you're talking to your wife. Operating only out of a micro-parenting mode, you may simply tell him to "shut up." You might even try to enforce this by spanking or striking him. Your child, because of fear or pain, may indeed quiet himself for the moment. And so it appears that this discipline technique actually worked.

But has it really? Not if you say to yourself, "W.A.I.T., What Am I Teaching?"

What *are* you really teaching a child when you hit him? You're teaching several things. Here are a few: 1) it's OK to hit another person, 2) it's OK to hit another person who is smaller than you, 3) it's OK to hit someone you love, 4) it's OK to hit someone when you feel angry or frustrated, 5) physical aggression is normal and acceptable under any circumstance, 6) Daddy can't control himself or his temper, 7) fathers are to fear, and 8) I must always be quiet in my father's presence.

If you go back and check the list of adult characteristics you want your child to learn, these aren't among them. Some men rationalize hitting a child by saying it teaches him or her respect. Actually, it doesn't. Look at the things listed above that a child really learns. Respect isn't one of them. Fear, anger, loathing for their fathers, and the power of physical aggression—these are what children learn. If you remember your true feelings after your father hit you, you'll agree.

Think about the neighborhood bully you knew as a kid. All he wanted was respect. How did you *really* feel about him? Respect probably doesn't come to your mind.

The use of violence in disciplining is one major way a child becomes alienated from his father. But alienation is not what we're after. We want to develop close, long-term, loving relationships. Building parent-child and child-parent respect starts with respecting the personhood of your child. And it requires living out your micro-parenting in direct relationship to your macro-parenting goals.

In actual practice, many fathers as well as mothers use spanking as a last resort. They may have tried one or two other methods first which did not work. "Work" in this sense means "work in the short term." For example, the child didn't stop crying, didn't stop unwanted behavior, or repeated something he shouldn't have done. Some parents, however, use spanking exclusively because they haven't learned other discipline techniques and it's what their parents did to them. Most feel guilty about this method even as they use it. "This hurts me more than it hurts you." Or they'll feel guilty about it after they've cooled down. And then they experience a vague sense of inadequacy.

There are, in fact, many constructive options you can apply to any discipline situation. A few are: give choices, distract the child, substitute activities, teach a skill, give encouragement, change your expectations, modify the environment, ignore minor misbehavior, anticipate problematic situations, use problem-solving communication, apply logical and natural consequences, provide time-outs, etc., etc.

The key is to learn what these options are, how to use them, and which work best with your child. For more information about discipline alternatives, consult the books listed under "Discipline" in Appendix D, Reference Book List. You can find several techniques you're comfortable using that work both in the short-term *and* the long-term. As a result, you will never reach the end of your list of methods, and thus never need "the last resort" of spanking.

Another way to look at this is to *do the second thing that comes to mind*. In most cases, the first thing you think of after misbehavior is some kind of physical punishment. Stop (W.A.I.T.). Acknowledge this as your first idea. Then let your mind take over. What discipline method will help you achieve your macro-parenting goals? Your second idea, then, will be the one to pursue. It also will be the one that builds, not tears down, family relationships.

••••

These are the basic road maps you will need throughout your fatherhood's journey. They detail your child's growth (temperament, stages, talents, and moods) and guide you through macro- and micro-parenting situations. So plan ahead. Secure these maps, study them, and keep them handy for quick reference.

CHAPTER 12

Road Hazards

Somewhere down the road, maybe sooner than you think, you will encounter one or more road hazards. Any of them could stall your fatherhood. However, if you know what to expect, the surprise factor is gone. And you'll be in a much better position to handle them.

Major Road Hazards

In your fathering, you will experience the following.

1. **Sleep deprivation.**

This is, perhaps, the one aspect of early parenting that surprises most fathers. Your image of a new baby is that he sleeps much of the time. This is true if you add up the total hours of sleep each day. But what you're not expecting is that it's usually in two-hour increments around the clock for the first few months.

This pattern is important because it results in parental sleep deprivation. You're not able to sleep undisturbed through the night. And there is no opportunity to catch up on missed sleep during the day. Maybe you can handle this for a few days. But not for weeks on end.

How do you behave when you're chronically tired? You're irritable. Small frustrations get to you more easily. Relationships are harder to handle. All of this occurs when you and your wife desperately need each other for support and encouragement. And it happens when you're anticipating great joy with a child whose limited wakefulness will create few demands.

So the contrast between what you "expected" and what "is" becomes quite sharp. This adds more frustration and heightened anxiety to your sleep-deprived situation.

2. **Helplessness.**

You enter parenting with a fair degree of self-confidence. You think, "How much trouble can a baby be? All he does is eat and sleep. If you put him in a crib, he can't climb out. So he's easy to control."

What actually occurs causes a blow to your self-esteem. Expect it. Parenting is not as easy as it looks or as you imagine. You may have had prior experience with other people's children. But this child is your total, 24-hour-a-day responsibility. You must learn to bathe, dress, hold, feed, burp, rock, diaper, comfort, and sing to him. You must figure out his temperamental preferences and moods. When you combine the responsibilities of baby care with your inexperience, you can feel an almost devastating sense of helplessness.

But sleep deprivation and helplessness are aspects of fathering that disappear with time and practice. As she grows, your infant is able to sleep for longer periods between feedings. Also, the more experience you get in caring for your baby, the more adept you become. You learn how to recognize and interpret her various cries. So you can diagnose her needs quickly and meet them. You're able to change a diaper with one hand tied behind your back (and a clothespin on your nose). And you become more relaxed in your parenting.

3. Changes in your relationship with your wife.

We've discussed how pregnancy, birth, and early parenting are crises. This is especially true for your marital relationship. No matter what kind of relationship you had in your B.C. life, it will certainly change A.C.

For one thing, your communication patterns change. At first, you and your wife may spend a great deal of time discussing the impending birth. Then after your baby arrives, you'll talk a lot about how to handle her. As a result, you'll find you have less and less couple-talk time. Even when you do make decisions as a couple, you may discover that the old solutions and compromises don't work anymore. Previously it may not have mattered if each of you had your own opinions. You sometimes "agreed to disagree." Now you must work together on the baby's care and upbringing. This creates a need for negotiation.

Secondly, your emotional life changes. Before children you and your wife developed a satisfying emotional life. You could rely on each other to "be there" when either needed support. But life with a young child can be so emotionally draining, there may not be sufficient energy left over for nurturing one another.

And thirdly, during early parenting your sex life definitely changes. You lose spontaneity. You must suspend sexual intercourse while your wife recuperates from childbirth. If your wife breast-feeds, her milk may begin to flow at awkward times. Sex has to be scheduled to coincide with your child's nap times, or for late at night when you're both exhausted. At best, it is always subject to interruptions and time or energy limitations. Furthermore, your wife could experience hormonal or emotional changes due to pregnancy and childbirth (such as post-partum depression) that affect your relationship. You may find that she simply isn't as interested in sex as an expression of your relationship or her sexuality. She may now view it as fulfilling different needs.

These potential changes affect the ways you and your wife relate to each other. They're true hazards to your marriage. And for many, these road hazards have caused not only uncomfortable rides but unfortunate crashes.

4. **Physical demands.**

As mentioned, early parenting is physically demanding. This aspect will last until your child is at least five years old.

At first you must carry your baby everywhere. But even mobile toddlers and preschoolers still need help dressing; going up and down stairs; being carried while asleep; and getting in and out of cribs, high chairs, and cars. This is not to mention all the wrestling, bouncing, rocking, and piggyback rides.

Also, you're constantly carrying toys or baby equipment wherever you go. At home, there's so much picking up and putting away of children's belongings that you soon discover the "true" meaning of the Bible verse, "When I became a man, I put away childish things."

5. **New complexity and number of relationships.**

This is one aspect of parenting no one truly realizes at first. But it's a further explanation for your stress or tiredness.

Before your child's birth, you and your spouse had basically two relationships: hers to you and yours to her. When your first child arrives, you don't just add one more relationship. You add several. You will now have: 1) yours to your wife, 2) your wife's to you,

3) yours to your child, 4) your child's to you, 5) your wife's to your child, 6) your child's to your wife, 7) yours to your wife and child's relationship, 8) your child's to you and your wife's relationship, and 9) your wife's to you and your child's relationship.

Because you love your wife and your child, you try to value and respect each relationship. The emotional energy it takes to do that can become exhausting. Now add a second child. How many relationships do you have then? How much more stress and tiredness?

Suffice it to say that adding one child may bless a couple but it certainly complicates life for them. And this additional complexity makes parenting more difficult than it first appears.

6. Change of lifestyle.

These previous road hazards all emphasize the fact that your life will very definitely change. Once you become a parent, there is no going back. It would be one thing if this change were gradual. But it's not. It comes upon you quickly, and usually without prior anticipation.

As a father, you're now responsible for a live human being. This is an awesome commitment in itself. Even when you're not in direct contact with your child, you're responsible for seeing that someone reliable and loving is. This means a new level of scheduling and decision-making in your life, and inevitably less spontaneity.

Because of these relentless responsibilities, you cannot live as you had been. You and your wife must now incorporate this new life into your family, creating a lifestyle that meets everyone's needs. This is why there is such a crisis nature to pregnancy and early parenting. This change goes through the entire fabric of your life— from superficial (buying diapers instead of a dinner out) to deeper issues (changing your job priorities). There's virtually no area of your existence untouched.

Further, lifestyle changes you may be expecting don't necessarily happen in reality. This is the frustrating thing. Each father enters parenting with some real and fantasy expectations. There are things you think will happen (your infant will sleep all night or she'll obey your every word). There are things you wish would happen (a smooth, fulfilling family life with no interruption to your career or personal lifestyle). And there are things you definitely don't want to happen (a cluttered home, a change in your sexual activity, or caring for a child with serious physical problems).

As a result you may feel smug about early parenting and your abilities to perform it. What comes your way, however, isn't necessarily what you expected. The actual changes never approximate your preconceived notions or your fantasies about what parenting will be like.

These discrepancies can contribute to a sense of failure, disappointment, dissatisfaction, or a rejection of your wife and child. But if you expect the unexpected, whatever happens will become a reality to deal with, not an unfulfilled fantasy to mourn.

7. Safety and health concerns.

These are deeply connected with the responsibility issue. New parents have much to learn about infant and toddler health and safety. This includes everything from physical health (how to take a baby's temperature) to emotional health (how to comfort a crying child). It also includes issues from environmental safety (babyproofing your home) to consumer safety (buying safe toys, cribs, or sleepwear).

Once your child becomes mobile, you'll discover all the ways tiny fingers and minds can get into things. You have to keep one step ahead to ensure your child's safety. This may mean getting door latches or installing that back fence. You learn to scan the environment as your child grows, anticipating new safety needs due to her changing skill levels.

In addition, you'll find that you must model good hygiene habits to your toddler or preschooler. This requires patient teaching and monitoring your own activities. You come to view your home and activities from a child's point of view in order to recognize and reduce unhealthy situations.

Being the parent of a small child also means frequent trips to the doctor's office. There are well-baby checkups; inoculations; and numerous visits for colds, rashes, ear infections, or other childhood illnesses. Also if your child participates in group care (whether daycare, preschool, church nursery, etc.), your family will probably share whatever colds and viruses those children pass around.

8. **Work issues.**

Fatherhood will have an unexpected impact on your overall career decisions.

It's normal to reevaluate your life in light of your new fatherhood. And one important aspect of your life is your career. In response to the financial needs and responsibilities of new parenthood, most men tend to require more from their jobs. They look for increased pay, wider benefits, or better job security. So now is a good time to determine whether your present job can meet these new needs created by your growing family. Discuss this with your wife. If she works outside the home, you must coordinate the financial and emotional impact of parenthood on both your jobs.

9. **Rapid growth and changes in your child.**

Within the first five years a child quickly grows from one age and stage into another. You barely get adjusted to how a one-year-old behaves, when the so-called "terrible twos" comes along. The three-year-old stage is a mere breather before the demands of life with a four-year-old. In the meantime, many milestones are taking place: teething, crawling, walking, talking, self-feeding, toilet training, and the like.

Often you hardly have time to catch your breath before adjusting to something new that's happening with your child. This is in addition to the many personal changes that you and your spouse are experiencing. It's yet another reason why early parenting is difficult.

10. **Pressures from other parents.**

There are others out there on the parental highways. Some can be hazardous to you. It's easy to get so caught up in dealing with them that you lose sight of why you are on the road in the first place.

For example, you may get hustled by the "speed" of parental peer pressure. You begin comparing your child's growth to that of your neighbor's child. Or perhaps you feel guilty about spending less money on your child than other fathers seem to do on theirs. Maybe you're concerned about how easy parenting looks for other people. These can all hook you into a competitive mode of fathering. You want others to see you as the ideal parent. But these feelings may divert your attention from your child's actual needs or growth, and from your loving relationship with her.

Your parents and in-laws can also create hazards. Most are well-intentioned, loving grandparents. And they can be helpful in giving assistance to new parents. But they're a roadblock if the assistance becomes interference, or they undermine your budding parental self-confidence. Only you and your wife can judge when that happens. In many cases, it occurs when they move beyond answering your requests for advice and begin telling you precisely how to raise your child(ren).

They may say, "I raised you this way and you turned out all right." In actuality, you might have another opinion about the quality of that child-rearing, since you were its recipient. Or the guilt you feel when they say that can make you uncritical of their ideas. The reality is it's been many years since they were new parents. They've forgotten a lot. Also research continues to add to our growing knowledge about child development. And the world your baby will live in, her safety needs, and the available equipment are very different. As a result, parenting approaches have changed. Listen to what your parents or in-laws have to say. Appreciate them for their good motives. Then intentionally decide with your wife what portion of it, if any, you will use.

Other fathers can also be a road hazard. As you know, there are many conflicting ideas about fatherhood. And there are men, especially influential ones at work, who will let you know their ideas. Some by their very silence about parenting may make you feel fatherhood isn't important. Others will show an interest in fathering in their conversations, but not follow through with their actions. And many men in management positions at work may discourage taking time off for family reasons. Or they will question your commitment to your career if you request it.

Along the way you will meet a variety of parents. This is why you must have a firm idea about what kind of father *you* intend to be. With this image constantly in mind, the road hazard of other parents becomes less of a problem on your journey.

••••

You should expect to encounter these ten major road hazards at any time or place. They can be very frustrating if they divert your attention from your family and hinder the progress of your relationships. You can't avoid them altogether. No one can. Instead you must be able to skillfully drive past them. Being flexible, performing problem-solving, exhibiting self-control, and understanding your child provide the means.

This is why using your road maps and learning how to operate your accelerator, gears, steering, and brakes are so important. Otherwise you could get off course, continually stall, or, even worse, wreck your fatherhood. If necessary, review Section III, Operating Your Fatherhood, with these road hazards in mind.

CHAPTER 13

Safe Driving Tips

Safety lies solely with you, the owner. You can operate your fatherhood in any manner you choose. It will go where you direct it, turn where you steer it, and stop when you apply the brakes. Thus *you* decide whether to operate it safely or not.

A Father's "Rules of the Road"

You will have a safer journey if you follow these tips.

1. **Obey speed limits.**

Going too fast is often more dangerous for your passengers than for you. Young children need to take life a little slower, a little easier, and a little simpler than adults. They must grow and develop at their own pace. In short, children need time to be children. If you're in too much of a rush, you'll miss the pleasures of fatherhood. And your passengers will feel anxiety instead of enjoying the ride.

2. **Adjust your speed to driving conditions.**

No matter how competent a driver you are or how well you plan your route, you will inevitably run into stormy weather. From time to time, we all have problems in our careers, marriages, parenting, family relationships, and so on. Slowing up and adjusting to a difficult situation can prevent a costly spin-out or crash.

3. Yield right-of-way.

It should be obvious that you are not the only one on the road. There are other parents who are trying to make a safe journey. You will also meet some reckless drivers who appear to have no sense of responsibility or concern for others.

Using defensive driving techniques (such as negotiation, problem-solving, and compromise) will help you get along better with other parents in your family, workplace, preschool, neighborhood, and religious group.

4. Drive with courtesy.

Patience and politeness are due to your passengers as well as to other drivers—whether they're on the road or stuck beside it. The Golden Rule applies: "Treat others as you would like them to treat you."

5. Signal lane changes.

Communication is important in all phases of life. Your fatherhood is no exception. Let others know *ahead of time* what your intentions and expectations are. You needn't make a big secret of the direction you want to take. Send out the signals that you're an active father and that you intend to properly operate your fatherhood. This allows others the opportunity to adjust and give you space. Then you'll be able to maneuver better, even in heavy traffic.

6. Use your mirrors.

Just as "objects in your mirror are closer than they appear," so are your immediate family members. Even though they may not communicate it, they really do love you. Acting independently of their needs and emotions can damage your relationships. Before you make sudden changes, look around. Ask yourself if you could possibly hurt a close loved one by your actions. Being deliberate in this way and avoiding any quick moves could prevent a great many problems.

7. Keep up with maintenance.

Many road accidents occur because of stalls, motor breakdowns, or flat tires. Simple preventative measures can eliminate the stress and pain of accidents. Refer to Section V to learn how to properly maintain your fatherhood.

8. Don't drink or do drugs and drive.

This should be obvious. There is no designated driver in real fatherhood. You're it.

9. Pay attention.

Fatherhood doesn't run by itself. You must attend to what you're doing. Be aware of events that occur around you. Watch for warning signals. If they light up, take care of the problem immediately. Become more informed about your journey. Regularly check your maps. Read the informational signs along the way and adjust your actions accordingly. Slow down for road hazards.

10. Allow sufficient time.

Operating your fatherhood under normal conditions takes time. However, you must allow extra time for any detours or hazards. If this is your first trip, you'll also want to provide for wrong turns and getting lost.

Speeding along just to get somewhere fast or first is not the object of fatherhood. The object is to enjoy the daily journey. The greatest gift you can give your family is your time.

Safe driving habits are just common sense. They help everyone. Incorporating them into your parenting style will keep you from adding to the wrecked fatherhoods already littering our city streets and country highways.

••••

END OF PART ONE

Part One of this Manual has given you the basic knowledge you need for safe, intentional, and satisfying operation of your new fatherhood. It's time now to put it into motion. After you've operated it for a while, refer to **Part Two**. It provides instructions for a preventative maintenance plan and vital tune-ups to keep your fatherhood in good working order.

-------PART TWO-------

SECTION V

MAINTAINING AND SERVICING YOUR FATHERHOOD

It's true in all aspects of life that for peak performance everything must be regularly maintained and serviced. You don't want your fatherhood relationships to break down through lack of attention. Instead, you want them in continuous operation so you can fully enjoy them. *Preventative Maintenance* and five periodic *Tune-ups* will keep your fatherhood functioning smoothly.

PREVENTATIVE MAINTENANCE

Many problems can be avoided altogether or their impact greatly diminished through a preventative maintenance program. Here's how to do it.

PERSONAL TUNE-UP

Personal Tune-ups will help keep you fit and your priorities in order.

MARITAL TUNE-UP

A Marital Tune-up encourages good communication. This, in turn, will deepen your relationship with your wife and strengthen your marriage.

FINANCIAL TUNE-UP

A Financial Tune-up can assist you in planning for your family's present and future needs. As a result, your economic base will be stronger.

PARENTAL TUNE-UP

A Parental Tune-up increases your parenting effectiveness as a couple through improved teamwork.

FAMILY TUNE-UP

Regular Family Tune-ups build a solid foundation for all your fatherhood relationships. You will experience less friction and enjoy more cooperation among family members.

CHAPTER 14

Preventative Maintenance

The concept of preventative maintenance is firmly fixed in our society. We've heard the saying, "An ounce of prevention is worth a pound of cure." We know from experience that the small cost of regular oil and lube jobs can prevent expensive car repairs. To get the most satisfactory crop from fruit trees we must prune, spray, and protect them from climate extremes ahead of time. We receive inoculations to avoid life threatening diseases. We brush and floss regularly to reduce the chances of tooth decay. Common wisdom dictates that a little effort now will prevent major problems later.

The purpose of your fatherhood's preventative maintenance program is to regularly monitor how your relationships are running. You can then identify and tackle problems while they are still relatively small. To do this you need to keep your senses alert. Listen for "squeaks," "rattles," or anything else unusual. Get a feel for whether the ride is becoming bumpier. Then search out the causes and do something about them.

Parts To Monitor

There are two areas of your fatherhood you should specifically focus on.

1. **Your engine.**

It's vital to keep your engine's four cylinders functioning well. That's where you will notice the beginnings of potential problems.

Pay specific attention to your Priorities Cylinder. This is the one that establishes family relationships as your top priority. And it unifies your other cylinders into an effective engine. It makes your *marriage* relationship the driving force for your Partnership Cylinder. Likewise it ensures that your *fathering* relationship is the core of your Parenting Cylinder. And in your Personal Growth Cylinder, it keeps your relationship with *yourself* central. So you can see how important it is to keep your Priorities Cylinder in good working order.

More often than not, any problem that comes up will occur within one of these three relationships. So if you hear an unusual "noise" or feel a "rub," the first thing to do is examine them.

Ask yourself, "In which one of my relationships is there an irritation?" Are you and your wife arguing more? Do you feel the need to be controlling? Are you unable to find enough time for your child? Are you feeling more stressed than usual, or sluggish and out of shape? These are just a few of the many questions you could ask to pinpoint a relationship problem.

Once you locate the problem area(s), review your values and priorities. No doubt you will reaffirm that you *want* to have a close, loving relationship with your wife. You *want* to develop a strong father-child bond. Or you *want* to be in good physical shape to keep up with the demands of work and fathering. Whatever your related values are, recommit yourself to them.

Finally, act on any changes necessary to realign yourself with your family relationships priority. Ask for forgiveness from your wife. Discuss areas of conflict and negotiate compromises. Re-evaluate your use of time so you can spend more of it with your child. Get more exercise. Put your work-life in line with your fathering values. And so on.

You don't want your fatherhood sitting useless on a rack. You want it out on the road. So make whatever adjustments it takes to eliminate problems while they're still small irritations.

2. **Your tires and shocks.**

If you're like most men, you expect more than operational power for your fatherhood's journey. You want a smooth ride regardless of the bumps and potholes you may encounter. For this you must look to your tires and shock absorbers. They are what give your fatherhood contact with the road of life.

It's important to keep your tires properly inflated. This will guarantee you better mileage and longer wear. Strong shock absorbers are also crucial because they even out the road, giving a more comfortable ride. They ensure that sudden, unexpected jolts won't make you lose control of your fatherhood.

Your overall *emotional stability and resilience* provide these needed fatherhood parts. The more attention you pay to them, the more satisfying the journey will be for you and everyone else.

Some men are very volatile in expressing their emotions. They show anger and violence at the least frustration. It seems that they constantly drive with emotionally worn tires and weak shocks.

Other men reject or repress their emotions almost entirely, so that no one knows what they're thinking or feeling. These men can't discuss feelings—whether their own or anyone else's. Since dealing openly with feelings is vital for healthy family relationships, their fatherhoods remain stranded up on blocks. They can't go anywhere because they have inadequate tires and shocks.

In between these two extremes are the rest of us. We can handle others' feelings most of the time. We can generally recognize and acknowledge how we feel. We can even have serious discussions on the subject. But in some cases we avoid dealing with the emotional complexities of life. As a result, we occasionally experience a rough ride in fatherhood. And deep down, we may feel disappointed in ourselves for not being able to handle emotions better.

Your Preventative Maintenance Plan

It is crucial for maintaining your fatherhood to develop an effective Father Support Network. The overall purpose is to let you know you're not alone. As mentioned, it's easy for new fathers to feel stress, loneliness, and a lack of confidence. Developing your Network is the antidote to those feelings and to the ways they drain the energy from your fatherhood.

There are groups to support you in practically every other aspect of your life—from hobby clubs to professional associations, from fraternal groups to religious congregations. Fatherhood, which is so significant in your life, needs support as well.

Here's how to develop your own Father Support Network.

1. Find and cultivate a mentor or two.

A mentor is a fellow father who is more experienced than you. Think of someone with stable relationships, who enjoys his fatherhood and can give you valuable insights. Look for someone who can grasp the whole picture, and guide you past the forks in the road and around the known trouble spots. Choose someone you trust. This could be your father, your father-in-law, another relative, a neighbor, co-worker, or friend. Develop an open relationship with him in which you feel comfortable discussing your fatherly ideas, feelings, and concerns.

2. Develop an informal network with other fathers.

If you took a childbirth class, that's a good place to start. Maybe you met some men there you felt comfortable with. You may know others in your neighborhood, at work, where you worship, or at your child's daycare or preschool. Encourage them to meet occasionally to discuss parenting matters. You might find they would welcome the opportunity for fatherhood shoptalk.

Be flexible, though. You could begin with an informal network that later spins off into a formal one. For example, one group of men met at their children's parent-cooperative preschool. They became friends and started getting together informally. Then their children graduated into grade school. At that point, they formed their own Indian Guide unit through the local Y.M.C.A. This enabled them to continue their father ties and schedule some father-child activities as well. Anything is possible.

3. Join an established group.

Ask around. Look in the "Community Events" section of your newspaper. Also check with your local hospital or social service agencies regarding parent support groups. You may find one that sponsors dad-child activities. Or it could be an adult support group for conversation. These organizations often bring in films, speakers, or other resources that an informal group may not be able to provide.

4. Enlist your spouse's support.

Your wife can be an excellent source of support. Discussing your fathering thoughts and feelings with her can help you clarify your goals. And since she's on the scene, she can provide valuable encouragement and feedback as you aim for those goals. Review Chapter 4, Partnership Cylinder, and check Chapter 18, Parental Tune-up.

5. Consult with professionals.

Your pediatrician is an excellent resource for child development and parenting information. Consult your personal physician about your own stress and energy concerns. Investigate evening parenting classes at community colleges or adult schools. And if the pressures of life bear down too hard, a family counselor can be extremely helpful in getting your fatherhood running again. Your pediatrician, doctor, pastor, rabbi, priest, Employee Assistance Program Counselor at work, or a local parental stress organization can refer you to an appropriate professional.

Benefits of a Father Support Network

A good Network ensures that your fatherhood will have the necessary emotional stability and resilience. This is how.

You become *accountable*. It's really not enough to have other fathers' companionship. You need the accountability that goes with it. Good friends encourage and support you. But they also speak straight. If they see you heading in a direction that's not good for you, they will say something. Because they care. You need to know that your fathering methods are accountable to other men whom you respect.

You receive *encouragement*. There are times when fatherhood and the decisions a father makes are very difficult. You need the support of other parents to keep your spirits up and your discouragement down. Often you may lack the courage to follow through on fathering as a high priority in your life. You need an input of courage, or "in-*courage*-ment." Likewise, you strengthen yourself when you encourage others.

You learn new *ideas.* Other parents and professionals can share their "tricks of the trade." They become a resource for different concepts, methods, or techniques. Their suggestions help you inject new life into your fatherhood and give you more efficiency. After all, no one wants to reinvent the wheel.

You gain *perspective*. This is a major gift other men can give you. In sharing their own experiences, they show you a different slant on any problem you have. Their objective viewpoints can help you realize that your problems are not unusual or unsolvable.

And finally, you have more opportunities for *sharing*. You need the friendship and perspective of other fathers. But you also need the chance to share your feelings with them. Without this vital and safe outlet, it's possible for negative emotions to build to explosive proportions.

••••

As a new father, you must adopt your own Preventative Maintenance Plan. By acknowledging that things can go wrong, you won't be surprised when small problems develop. Your Plan, then, will help you monitor your fatherhood's functioning and take care of these problems as they occur—instead of ignoring them until they cause a major breakdown.

CHAPTER 15

Personal Tune-Up

Even if you have a preventative maintenance program in place, eventually something gets out of adjustment and needs a tune-up. This is not unusual. Wear and tear happens to all moving parts—whether they're in an appliance or a relationship. It doesn't mean that those parts were faulty. There need be no value judgement placed on such wear. It's just something that occurs through use.

The first area in which you will need to perform occasional tune-ups is your *personal* life.

Simply put, *you* are your fatherhood's body. The condition of your fatherhood reflects the condition of your personal life. Because this is such an important area, it must not be ignored. The recommended schedule is to take a look at yourself every six months in the following two areas: *self-esteem* and *personal health*.

Self-Esteem

Basically, self-esteem refers to how you view yourself. If you constantly put yourself down, worry about your work performance, think you can't do what it takes to be a good father, believe that you're a poor husband, or complain that you can't communicate your feelings—you have *low* self-esteem.

On the other hand, if you feel comfortable with yourself as a husband and father, think of yourself as competent at your job, enjoy a challenge, or are successfully learning to deal with your feelings—then you have a *higher* self-esteem.

Good self-esteem is important for effective fathering. It gives you the confidence to drive into new areas and gain more experience. It gives you the stamina to persist in learning the many new skills you need as a father. And it gives you the sensitivity and strength to be a nurturing person.

Good self-esteem also gives you the courage to just say "No!" "No" to those opportunities or people who would keep you from being the father you want to be. "No" to those feelings that urge you to be unfaithful to your marriage relationship. "No" to those situations that place something else above your family relationships priority. "No" to peer pressure that would make you deny your commitment to good fathering. "No" to your own thoughts that hinder a realistic perspective on life. "No" to letting job demands split your family rather than support it.

It's quite easy as a new father to develop low self-esteem. The unanticipated pressures on your marriage and job, your physical and emotional fatigue, and your lack of experience in caring for your child can all contribute to insecure feelings. This is why it's very important to regularly examine your self-image and take steps to re-tune it when necessary.

Another self-esteem problem occurs when a man confuses his identity (who he is) with his job or career (what he does to make money). These are two, very separate things.

When a man defines himself by his job, this is what he's thinking: "If I could get promoted to a higher position, make more money, or have greater prestige, I will be loved and respected by my wife, my family, my father, and everyone else." So he puts extra time and effort into his job in order to "be somebody" to the detriment of his close relationships. Often when he has achieved the desired career level, money, or prestige, he feels unfulfilled. Something is still missing from his life. His self-esteem is still low. And he wonders what it takes to find fulfillment.

Searching for identity in the work arena is futile. Gaining higher self-esteem and personal fulfillment starts with finding yourself in your *relationships* with your wife, child(ren), other family members, friends, and your God.

To accomplish this, consider these:

- Review your life's priorities. Recommit yourself to setting *relationship goals* and following personal and career lifestyles that reflect or support them.
- Discover what triggers your insecure feelings (particular events, work cycles, physical stress, etc.). When you know their source, you can respond to them more effectively.
- Deepen your relationship with your wife and family by spending more time together and openly sharing your feelings.
- Talk to people in your Father Support Network to get a different perspective on any troubling parenting situation.
- Consult some good books on child development to increase your knowledge about growth and normal behavior, as well as to pick up parenting tips. See Appendix D, Reference Book List.
- Regularly do something you're good at (music, hobbies, athletics, etc.). Reaffirm to yourself that you have special skills and abilities.
- Look for ways to reward yourself for learning something new, persevering through a tough time with your child, or finding a more satisfying way to communicate with your wife.
- Begin, renew, or deepen your spiritual commitment and faith life.

Personal Health

The stresses, responsibilities, and sheer physical demands of fatherhood can take their toll on your energy level, immune system, and sexual enjoyment. As a new father it's more crucial than ever to maintain your overall personal health. Here are effective ways.

1. **See your doctor regularly.**

Whatever your age, this is vital for every man. It's just common sense. Yet in practicing physical maintenance, many of us fall short. According to our machismo attitude, we ought to "work through the pain." It's also difficult for many of us to divulge anything personal about ourselves, let alone confront the possibility of our mortality. And a physical exam is very personal. We may believe that we wouldn't be able to cope with what was found. The doctor might ask us to give up something we enjoy or think we need. Or perhaps we're just too busy with our careers to take time out for checkups, especially when we feel fine.

Nevertheless, the older you get, the more important regular visits to the doctor are. Consult with your physician to see how often you should schedule exams. And then put them on your calendar. Do the same for dental and vision checkups.

2. **Exercise.**

Look around. Many men begin to "go to pot" when they become fathers. Their middles start to spread. They tire more easily. Or they get muscle sprains more often. We all share these experiences to one degree or another.

While you're at the doctor's office, ask about what exercise programs are best for you and your lifestyle. With the proper regimen, you can start to firm up and actually gain more energy. The time you allocate to regular exercise will pay great dividends for your marriage, fatherhood, and career as well.

3. **Examine your diet.**

An integral part of good physical health is a proper diet. Again, check with your doctor. Elevated cholesterol levels and the potential for heart problems occur even in young men. You may need a diet lower in fat, or one with more vegetables, fruit, or fiber. Changing your diet and exercising regularly will help reduce your flab and fatigue. The earlier you can detect and respond to any problem, the better it will be for you and your family.

4. **Reduce stress.**

Find the sources of stress in your life and do something about them *now* before they create medical problems.

Learn how to reduce stress on a *daily* basis. Exercise and diets are big helps. You can also try deep breathing or relaxation techniques. Use your Father Support Network or call a Parental Stress Hotline to talk things out. Enjoy hobbies or other forms of play. Take proper vacations or regular mini-vacations to recharge your battery. After all, a fully charged battery helps your engine function properly. Recognize your limitations. Develop the ability to control the effect of negative thoughts. Do some "positive visualization" (much like an athlete does before an important meet or game). Apply time management principles to your work and personal schedule.

5. Attend religious services of your choice.

These will help you grow in your faith and religious beliefs. They will strengthen the connections to your roots and higher values. They will enable you to put your life into perspective and your priorities in order. You can also develop your Father Support Network among the people you meet there.

6. Get intellectual stimulation.

Just as you must exercise your body or spirit, you also need to exercise your mind. Seek activities that will help you develop your intellect—even if it's as simple as reading the daily newspaper to keep current on world events. Read books, visit museums, attend musical performances, investigate historical sites, take a class, or watch some educational TV shows.

7. Develop safety awareness.

Whether you're at home, leisure, or work, being aware of safety issues makes good sense. One misjudgment or careless move can injure your back, break an arm, or worse. Any one of these can put you and your fatherhood out of action in a flash.

••••

As you regularly perform this Personal Tune-up, you may discover other adjustments specific to your needs. Whether you do or not, improving your self-esteem and personal health will keep your fatherhood moving.

CHAPTER 16

Marital Tune-Up

Regular Marital Tune-ups are fundamental for maintaining a healthy relationship with your wife. It is recommended that you perform a Marital Tune-up every six months, but certainly no less than once a year.

This Tune-up is one you and your wife should consciously plan together. It means that both of you agree to a meeting time and place, mark your family calendar, and follow through. However, if you have an argument right before the meeting, you may want to postpone your Tune-up for a few days. Your heightened emotions could sidetrack constructive work.

This special time together requires childcare. You cannot perform a meaningful Marital Tune-up when you're distracted by or responsible for your child. There will be too many interruptions to your conversation.

The focus of this Tune-up is not on either person's problems or characteristics. It's on the *quality* of your marital relationship. This relationship is the foundation for your family life and positive childraising. So as you live out your marriage, you not only want to *preserve* its quality but *strengthen* it.

Examine Your Relationship

There are three basic areas you should look at during each Tune-up.

1. The quality of your teamwork.

A marriage relationship is a special one. By nature, it's more than merely a love relationship. The law recognizes it as a legal contract. Government sees it as a business with shared assets. Employers view it as worthy of additional benefits. The religious community celebrates it as a sacred, lifelong commitment.

Your mutual lifestyle rests on the quality of your marriage and how it actually *works*. For example, you must cooperate to nurture one another, rent or own a home, earn and spend money, establish credit, maintain your living area, own cars, and buy insurance—not to mention conceive and raise children. If you have problems working together, the overall quality of your home-life diminishes.

The key to a quality relationship is to understand that *good team members are equal in importance*. While each person may have his or her own interests and skills, they work together for the good of the team. The team's needs come before an individual's desires.

There are two steps to creating good teamwork. First, both of you must *work at and achieve open communication.* This means being able to discuss your feelings and thoughts honestly, as well as carefully listening to and understanding those of your spouse. In many cases, just being sounding boards for one another can be a valuable end in itself. However, this kind of communication is different than conversations that seek a specific solution to a problem. At the beginning of any discussion, be sure each person knows what kind of communication you will engage in. Also, discuss definitions of key concepts.

And second, the two of you must *negotiate mutually agreeable solutions.* This is the step that's most often missed. You can talk until you're both exhausted. You can clearly understand each other's feelings and positions. But if you don't take the next step and work out compromises for your disagreements, you've gained very little. Your relationship doesn't move forward. This second step is what will improve your marital teamwork.

You are partners. You are a *team.* If either of you feels this is not the case, then where you got off course and how you can remedy it should be an area of focus in your Tune-up.

2. The nature of your mutual support.

This is closely related to being a team player, but it goes deeper. Marriage is ideally a relationship in which two adults personally support one another through everything life brings. Remember your wedding vows about "for richer or poorer, in sickness and in health," etc.?

One major aspect of personal support is *emotional support.* It's very important to be sensitive to your spouse's feelings and ideas. Each needs to take the other seriously—not tease, condescend, or ridicule. When either person believes this isn't being done, there's a serious breach in the emotional relationship. You can use the communication process described in Chapter 4, Partnership Cylinder, to achieve a mutual understanding of feelings.

Gaining a deeper knowledge of your spouse's various stages of personal development will also help you provide emotional support. One excellent way to get a long-term perspective on your wife is to envision her as a dynamic person who will continue to grow and change well into old age. She will be susceptible to varying pressures, difficulties, and frustrations as she grows through the seasons of her life. Viewing her in this way will increase your understanding of your wife. And it will help you support her in times of trouble, as well as celebrate with her in times of joy.

Another major aspect of mutual personal support is *career support*. Discovering how each of you can encourage and strengthen the other in your individual careers (whether this means working outside or inside the home) is another topic for your Marital Tune-up. This can be a delicate subject for both of you, but it requires discussion.

You may find that your working lives will develop unevenly through the years. At any given time, one person's career may be at a crucial stage, while the spouse's isn't. Later on, it could be the other way around. Perhaps one of you has been laid off or is going through a tough time at work. Maybe a change in job responsibilities or supervisors has brought new headaches. That person needs extra support during this period. At some point, one of you may be considering a complete career change. If you both agree it's necessary, you will need to discuss how to support one another through the process. However, what one might perceive as support may not be how the other defines it (remember the card game of LOVE). Clear communication is the key.

3. The depth of your reciprocal love.

Discuss this last, not first. If you can't work together as a team and provide mutual support, you're not going to feel love. Marriage therapists know that negative teamwork and support issues interfere not only with a good sex life but with the ability or desire to exchange basic gestures of affection.

Affection and sex are closely linked in a marriage relationship. This doesn't mean that one automatically leads to the other. It means that in a lifestyle where genuine affection does not exist, neither does meaningful sex.

If you and your wife are experiencing an unsatisfactory sex life, first discuss any issues regarding teamwork and mutual support.

Review how each of you defines "giving and receiving affection" and "a satisfactory sex life." Talk about how each can show more affection daily so it will be understood as an expression of love. Then you're ready to discuss your physical sex life. Decide precisely what you *both* can do to improve it—starting tonight (or this weekend). This communication process, done in an atmosphere of caring and mutual respect, will help you see exactly which areas of your relationship need a Tune-up.

In the beginning, a particular way your wife experiences love may not be one of your ways (which was the husband's initial difficulty with giving diamond cards in the game of LOVE). At most, it can be completely foreign to you. At the least, you could feel slightly awkward doing or saying it. However, consider it as your *gift* to her. This will help you create a good environment for communicating your love.

Make Adjustments

The basic concept of a Tune-up is not that something needs to be scrapped but that it needs adjustment. Or, put another way, some aspect of your relationship requires a mid-course correction to keep your marriage headed in the right direction. Once you've discussed an issue and decided on a specific change, your next step is to make that change a part of your lifestyle.

Ask yourself, "What factors in our lives will *hinder* this new way of relating to one another? And what will *support* it?" These questions help you focus on specific areas in order to implement the changes you want. Then work together to strengthen those parts of your lives that would support or improve your desired relationship. Reduce those aspects that would weaken it. In other words, accentuate the positive and eliminate the negative.

For example, perhaps you and your wife decide that going out more as a couple will improve the quality of your marriage. You can strengthen this decision by agreeing to set aside a specific time for dates, such as the last Saturday of each month. Making reservations will reinforce your commitment. Or you could buy tickets in advance for an event you'd both enjoy. Then if either person is tired or wavering, the other can say, "We've already spent the money. It would be a shame to waste it."

You can further support your decision by keeping a family calendar on which you schedule dates for three or four months in advance. Protect these couple-times as you would an appointment with your boss, or tickets for a pro football game. If an opportunity comes up to do something else that night, refer to your calendar and respond, "Sorry I'm booked. How about next week?"

A hindrance to your plan might be the lack of good childcare. To weaken or eliminate this negative factor, check with friends, family, and neighbors for new babysitting leads. Or join a babysitting co-op. You can also make backup plans for childcare so your dates aren't sacrificed if your baby or sitter becomes ill.

••••

Paying attention to the quality of your teamwork, the nature of your mutual support, and the depth of your love will help keep your marriage relationship in tune. And you'll find a lot more harmony and enjoyment in all aspects of your life together, including your fathering. This is well worth your effort in the long run.

CHAPTER 17

Financial Tune-Up

The reason for monitoring your finances is quite simple. All your family relationships require *financial* as well as emotional support. You have basic needs for food, clothing, shelter, utilities, transportation, childcare, medical care, household goods, and entertainment. If possible, you should establish a savings account to help you meet unexpected bills or periodic major expenses. For financial stability, you will also want insurance—health, life, auto, home, and disability.

A Financial Tune-up is recommended at least once a year. Some good times to do it are: January 2 (to prepare for the calendar year), April 16 (after tax time when records are handy), September 1 (after summer vacation expenses), or December 1 (before the holiday spending).

During each Financial Tune-up session, you and your spouse must *work together* to develop your family spending philosophy and priorities. It's when financial issues aren't discussed thoroughly and agreed on that couples run into problems. Marriage therapists report that in many cases, financial disagreements (not problems with sex, in-laws, careers, or children) are what cause the divorce rate to climb. So when conducting a Financial Tune-up, you both should exercise good listening, communicating, and negotiating skills.

Choose a time for your meeting. Mark it on your family calendar to reserve the date. Make sure you allot at least a couple of hours. A half day or less should be sufficient under normal circumstances. Hire a babysitter so you'll have no interruptions. Or exchange childcare time with a neighbor or friend.

Since finances can be a touchy subject, set discussion ground rules before you begin. These might include: stick to the issue, no name-calling, no recriminations, no interrupting, work together on solutions, make decisions by consensus, abide by what's decided, and the like.

Performing the Tune-Up

There are four major areas you'll want to cover.

1. Financial status overview.

Get out your financial records—recent pay stubs, bank statements, mortgage information, credit card statements, etc.

Figure out your family's annual after-tax income. Divide it into a monthly amount. Now you know what disposable income your family is actually bringing in. This is your net monthly income. You may not want to consider interest income as part of this figure. Instead you might prefer to estimate it for the year and use it for a pre-selected purpose, special event, or holiday activities.

Now list your debts. Include car, house, credit card, or other loan payments. Calculate a monthly figure for your debt as well. This is the monthly outgo you're responsible for in addition to monthly living expenses (food, clothing, transportation, utilities, insurance, etc.).

Compare your combined monthly outgo and living expenses to your net monthly income. This lets you see at a glance how stable your finances are.

While you're at it, it's a good idea to monitor how you are handling your resources. Examine the status of your checking and savings accounts. Is your checking account constantly overdrawn? If so, why is this happening? Is it simply overspending? Or is it a cash flow problem due to the timing of your paychecks and major bills or debt payments? Are you able to add to savings regularly? What's the status of each credit card? Is it being overused? Hint: the answer is yes if you frequently pay interest charges. Examine what you're paying out yearly in credit card interest for all accounts combined. Is it adding too much to your debt picture?

Based on all this, determine your current financial status. Has it changed since your last Financial Tune-up? If so, why? Do you have different jobs, higher or lower income, more or less debt, another child, another car, unexpected medical expenses, or a newly purchased home or appliance?

After you've done this a few times, getting a financial overview becomes easier. You're able to notice and do something about negative trends.

If you feel your financial situation is getting out of control, consult with a financial planning expert. Look under the heading Financial Planning in your phone book's business pages. However, be sure to check qualifications, references, and areas of expertise carefully. Financial Planners are not licensed or regulated by public agencies. Someone in your Father Support Network, an accountant, or a lawyer may be able to refer you. An experienced Financial

Planner can help you even if your affairs are not out of control but you just need good advice.

2. Budget.

If you don't have a monthly family budget, make one *now*.

List all of the categories in which you spend money. These could include: car expenses, charitable donations, child(ren), clothing, college savings, debt reduction (credit cards, loans, etc.), education, entertainment, family activities, food, gifts, holiday expenses, home maintenance, household utilities, insurance, medical/dental, miscellaneous, phone, rent/mortgage, retirement, savings, taxes, and vacation. Keep track of your expenses for at least six months, including some winter ones (12 months is best). Using these figures, compute your average monthly expenditures by category (divide the total spent in each category by the number of months for which you kept records). Then put the categories and the monthly averages down in a log.

The total of your average monthly expenditures for all categories is your monthly outgo. Now check this against your net monthly income. How do the bottom lines compare? If your outgo is higher, you need to reduce spending in some categories or even delete others to get your budget in line. This means discussing priorities in your current lifestyle. Unlike the Government, a family cannot survive deficit spending for very long.

You may have some new expenses since your last Financial Tune-up. This will require adding other categories to your record-keeping in order to budget for them. Or you might have received a raise. Change the numbers in your log accordingly, until your monthly outgo is in line with your net income. This revision, then, becomes your current budget until your next Financial Tune-up. If you have a computer, there are good software programs available to help with this process.

3. Spending philosophy.

You and your wife must be committed to the goal of financial stability in order to achieve it. An effective budget is a means to that goal. But you must also discuss and agree on a joint spending philosophy in order to make your budget work. It's a team effort.

Perhaps one of you is an impulse buyer, and the other likes to research purchases first. Maybe one person believes strongly in building a savings account, while the other wants to spend now. Or one spouse may rely solely on credit cards, and the other prefers to use cash. Whatever your thoughts are about money matters, it's best to get them out on the table for discussion and negotiation.

The key is that, despite differences in habit, both of you must agree to abide by the budget. This may mean making compromises in your spending philosophies.

4. Related business matters.

Financial Tune-ups are also good times to investigate, discuss, and decide on several items of family business. For example, use this opportunity to decide what records need to be saved for tax purposes, and where to put them. Find out if either of you can get your paycheck deposited directly into your bank account. Check on whether your employers have credit unions which will automatically deposit savings before you receive your paychecks. Discuss renting a safety deposit box in which to store your will or valuable personal items. Ask whether your employer has any tax saving benefits for your medical, dental, or life insurance premiums. And see if there's a program at work that allows you to use pre-tax earnings for childcare or eldercare costs.

You may also want to set future financial goals. You can choose short-term goals (from one to four years) to pay off your credit card debts, build an emergency fund, or increase your insurance coverage. Medium-term goals (from five to ten years) could help you finance a special trip, new car, or home remodeling. While long-term goals (beyond ten years) will help you put the children through college or retire early. The nature of these goals will dictate what kind of career, savings and/or investment plans you decide to develop together.

••••

In all aspects of your marriage, it's important that both you and your wife function as a team. Regular Financial Tune-ups will help you work together for family stability instead of pulling in opposite directions.

CHAPTER 18

Parental Tune-Up

One of the first things you realize as a father is that neither you nor your wife will automatically know what to do in every parenting situation. You find yourselves driving blind a lot of the time. And it can be scary. This is why it's recommended that you have a Parental Tune-up once a month. These Tune-ups work best when your child is sleeping or another person is caring for her. Then you and your wife can talk without interruptions.

Tune-Up Agenda

During a Parental Tune-up, you may want to do some or all of the following.

1. **Discuss your needs and feelings as parents.**

You and your wife need opportunities to express your feelings about parenting. Perhaps you're frustrated because you're trying to change your child's behavior, but nothing seems to work. Maybe you're angry at your wife because of a difference in your parenting styles, or because she always seems to correct your ways of handling the baby. You might be tired of the constant demands your baby makes on your time, patience, and energy. Or anticipating a change in your child's development (more mobility, teething, "terrible twos," toilet training, etc.) could be making you anxious. Whatever the problem is, you both need to share your feelings.

This doesn't mean having an argument. It means that each person will give the other uninterrupted time to speak honestly and without recriminations.

You can also state what you think would help to resolve a problem. For example, you may want more time with your child. Or you may need a buffer period between getting home from work and playing with or caring for your baby. This is the time to let your spouse know what's on your mind.

But remember, it's an opportunity for two-way communication, not for accusation and demands. Once you've heard your wife's thoughts and feelings and expressed your own, you're both ready to work on meeting each other's needs.

2. Note changes or growth in your child.

Children develop so quickly, especially in the early years, that it's hard to keep current. It seems that one day your daughter is teething, and the next she's walking. Or your son, who used to smile at everyone a few weeks ago, now starts to cry if grandma picks him up. One week you can put your baby on the living room floor and feel confident that she won't go anywhere. Soon thereafter, she's able to pull breakables off the coffee table.

Both you and your wife need to be alert to changes in your child, *no matter how subtle.* One major reason is to vary your parenting approach in response to new growth. It's also important because sudden changes in a child's demeanor or behavior could indicate physical, emotional, or relational problems. You'll want to consult with your pediatrician if you notice anything unusual.

3. Identify your child's idiosyncrasies.

Your child is a unique person. She's not a miniature version of you or your wife. She's not a carbon copy of your other child(ren). Nor is she the child of your dreams, the perfect baby you've fantasized about or anticipated raising. She's an individual from birth. You cannot plan or predict what temperament your child will have.

Your child will "tell" you his idiosyncrasies through his behavior—his favorite kinds of play, the way he adapts to changes, his eating preferences, his moods, his balance between active and quiet periods, and so on. By observing your child, you will come to understand him better. Is he quiet and cautious about new activities? Is he boisterous, active, inclined to dramatize his emotions? What is peculiar to him as a person? Let your wife know when you think you see another of your child's personal traits. Talking about them gives you both a more accurate picture of your child, and helps you better handle old problems or new behavior.

4. **Put your child's present behavior into the context of his long-range needs.**

This is one of the most important things to discuss. What are the long-term needs of your child? Review the micro-parenting and macro-parenting concepts discussed in Chapter 11, Road Maps.

Sometimes we overreact on the issue of long-term goals. When we see our one- or two-year-olds grab toys, refuse to share, and hit or bite other children, we fear they'll grow up to be antisocial. We often think our children should embody every positive trait, even from the beginning. When we observe that they don't, we may panic. Actually, it takes years of practice and many mistakes for a child to develop into a mature, sensitive person with good social skills.

On the other hand, we can underestimate the importance of long-term goals. It's clear that a child's long-range needs should impact decisions about his present behavior and care. For example, look at the studies of children's TV or video watching. Research shows that extensive viewing time during the preschool years has a negative effect on the child's development of relational skills. It also decreases his academic skills later. Thus parents who are concerned about teaching those skills must strictly monitor and direct their children's TV viewing habits from the beginning.

We can encourage positive growth by consistently guiding our children in the right direction. But as parents, we don't have any idea of that direction unless we have considered and agreed upon our children's long-range needs. When discussing these needs, however, be sure to talk about your actual child—not a male or female stereotype, or some ideal baby.

5. Discuss the handling of specific events.

Before you decide how to handle problem behavior, it helps if you and your wife compare observations about your child's growth, needs, and idiosyncrasies.

Then evaluate the event or behavior in question. Ask yourselves, "What was our child *really* doing? How can we understand the situation better? What were the environmental factors (time of day, noise level, social interactions, etc.)? What parenting methods have we already tried? Did any work to our satisfaction? What are our second thoughts? How can we improve our response?"

At this point you can do some research. Consult childraising books that talk about the problem. You'll find some excellent resources in Appendix D, Reference Book List. Read about and discuss what is considered the *normal* range of behavior and needs for your child's age. This will help you and your wife put the

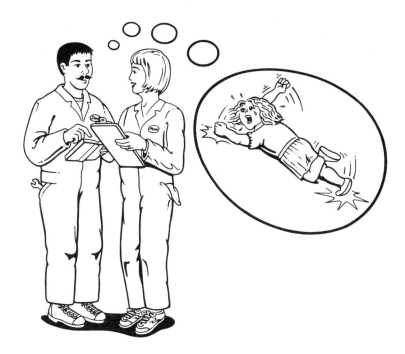

problem into perspective. It will increase your options for responding, and help you decide which to use. You can anticipate the
expected effects on your child. And you will greatly reduce your
parental frustrations.

This kind of problem-solving puts both you and your spouse on
the same team and helps establish consistent parenting. Consis-
tency is emotionally reassuring for your child. It also prevents him
from playing one parent against the other.

Benefits of Parental Tune-Ups

By using these discussion ideas as guidelines, you can develop
your own style of Tune-ups to suit your specific parental concerns.
But why go through all this? After all, parenting is time and labor
intensive enough without extra discussions and research.

Because it works. There are several benefits from performing
regular Parental Tune-ups. Here are a few you will find once you've
tried them.

The Parental Tune-up habit encourages you to *discuss childraising methods and philosophies* with your wife. By talking these
over, you share each other's thoughts, concerns, and experiences.
You get to know one another better and even develop insights into
each other's childhoods. You can also clarify or alter goals and
plans more easily to reflect your current family dynamics and
values.

You can *discuss your child rationally*. Many times parents
disagree in front of their child about each other's method of
handling a problem. Of course, this is no time to be debating
parental techniques. Such discussions or criticisms can quickly
deteriorate into arguments. The child gets a confused message
about his undesired behavior. So it is likely to be repeated. However, in a Parental Tune-up you're removed from the emotional
situation. You can calmly and rationally talk about whatever
parental differences you might have without undermining each
other. And this leads to better solutions for both parents and child.

Regular Tune-ups help you both *keep up-to-date on your child's growth*. You and your wife observe and interact with your child in different ways, at different times, and under varied circumstances. This is because you're unique persons in your own right. Therefore, you will see behavior that your spouse might not have noticed yet. And vice versa. Sharing observations will give both of you a more complete picture of your child.

Parental Tune-ups are invaluable if you're trying to *overcome stereotypes*. By discussing each other's assumptions about children and parenting techniques, you can spot ways you may be stereotyping your child or yourselves. This helps you change more quickly to childraising methods appropriate for your family.

You take the opportunity to *brainstorm and/or research answers* to your problems. Through reading or consultation with your pediatrician, you can learn what is normal for children at different developmental stages. This helps you relax about changes you've noticed in your child. Understanding what your child can and can't do at each stage of growth will assist you in planning age-appropriate activities. Plus you will discover a variety of new parental approaches and techniques to try. Your new knowledge will increase your confidence as a parent. And you will build a better repertoire of parenting tools.

Finally, you can *work out a flexible, common parenting plan*. When you jointly decide on what approach you're going to take, you will experience a real sense of relief. Of course, this doesn't mean your plans will always work. You might have to change your methods later. But that's up for discussion at your future Parental Tune-ups.

••••

Parental Tune-ups help you and your wife give each other something so needed in parenting today—*moral support*. It's hard enough being a parent. But it's harder still if you're working against each other or feel like you're doing it alone. Regular Parental Tune-ups will help you function as a team and make parenting easier as you go along.

CHAPTER 19

Family Tune-Up

> **NOTE: Begin Family Tune-ups toward the end of your child's preschool years, when he is an articulate four- or five-year-old. This kind of Tune-up is described now so you can use it when your child is ready.**

 Practically everything that happens to you has a direct effect on your family. This is certainly true of any changes resulting from your Personal, Marital, Financial, and Parental Tune-ups. Because of your family relationships priority, you will want to make sure that your family life runs as smoothly as possible. And your family members should have the opportunity to plan activities, discuss changes, or solve problems that affect them. Family Tune-ups, in the form of *weekly* Family Meetings, will promote this kind of cooperation and communication.

Establishing Your Family Meetings

Here's how to get started.

1. Agree on the general purpose of the Meetings.

Meetings provide a forum to talk about anything that affects your family or how it operates. For instance, you can use this time to discuss and solve any family problems that arise. These could range from household chores and teasing siblings, to allowances or new bedtimes. You can also plan family events like birthdays, picnics, vacations, special dinners, holiday celebrations, or any other fun times.

Family Meetings are opportunities to strengthen family unity. You might want to encourage someone in the family who is struggling with change or has suffered a recent disappointment. Or you could recognize achievements of individual family members. For example, you or your wife may have received a raise. Or perhaps your child learned a new skill, completed a difficult task, or earned an award. You can verbalize your love and congratulations to each person individually, and plan a special family celebration at the Meeting.

2. Keep a positive attitude.

Meetings are not a time for arguments, recriminations, or complaints about the children. It is essential that you see your Meetings as a forum to improve family relationships, increase communication, and find effective solutions to problems. Viewed this way, your family will reap benefits from these Meetings throughout your parenting years and beyond.

3. Pick a time to meet.

Set a regular day and time of the week (for example, every Sunday night right after dinner, every Saturday morning at 10:00 a.m., or every Wednesday evening at 7:00 p.m.). Select a time that's convenient for all family members, and when people won't be distracted by other responsibilities or feel too tired. Of course, the younger your child is, the more limited are the times you can choose.

Mark Meeting dates for the next six months on your family calendar. This will help you reserve the time so nothing will interfere with the Meetings. If postponement of a Meeting is absolutely necessary, immediately agree on a new date and enter it. Try to avoid changing or cancelling Meetings, because family members will soon depend on this forum to make their needs known and resolve difficulties.

4. Pick a place to hold your Meetings.

Choose a comfortable place where there will be no distractions. One of the best is your kitchen or dining room table. Sitting around a table communicates unity. It also encourages equal participation from all family members. Before the Meeting begins, clear the table of everything. And most importantly, turn off the radio, stereo, or TV.

5. Agree on the Meeting's length.

When your child is still a preschooler, he can only participate on a basic level. The Meeting will need to be very short. Limit the agenda to a single issue with a simple decision.

A five-year-old (especially an articulate one) can handle a longer Meeting with a few subjects. However, because your child's attention span is still not well developed, Meetings should last no more than 15 to 20 minutes.

6. Agree on a general agenda.

There's a difference between a family gathering and a Family Meeting. It has to do with the purpose and structure of the get-together. In a family gathering, conversation is general and spontaneous with a free flowing give-and-take. People enter or leave the group on a casual basis. A Family Meeting, however, is a more formal time to deal with particular family issues. Everyone attending a Meeting must agree this is why he or she is there.

This formality is reflected in an actual agenda. At first you may want to deal with just "New Business" (this weekend's picnic, or celebrating your child's learning to tie his shoes). As you gain more experience, you can add "Old Business" (the ongoing discussion of allowances, or a problem that wasn't resolved at the last Meeting). Later, you may decide to add other elements, such as a time of recognition for each family member.

The key is to plan what works best for your family. However, there definitely needs to be structure for your Meetings. And there should always be a balance between problem-solving and planning family fun times so that the Meetings are upbeat.

7. Establish a running agenda.

Ideas for family activities, achievements to celebrate, and complaints or problems to discuss will surface between Meetings. Put them on a list. The refrigerator door is an ideal place for it. These issues or ideas will then form the coming Meeting's agenda. Just knowing that a problem will be dealt with at the next Meeting can relieve angry feelings about it in the meantime.

8. Rotate the leadership of your Meetings.

There are two leadership positions: Moderator and Recorder. The Moderator calls the Meeting to order, and announces or asks for agenda items. He or she keeps the Meeting running smoothly by ensuring that everyone is able to talk without interruptions or criticisms. The Recorder enters every final decision, agreement, or planned activity into the Meeting's log.

At first, of course, you and your wife need to rotate these duties. But increasingly you should encourage your child's participation. During her early grade school years, she will be able to start taking a turn as Moderator. Once she prints well, you can help her log decisions as the Recorder.

Family Meetings are an excellent teaching opportunity. You're helping your child learn at an early age how to work in a group, express needs and feelings, use problem-solving skills, and develop compromise strategies. Just as your child's first staggering steps eventually lead to running, these basic social skills will be refined and strengthened over the years. Imagine the leadership skills your children will have in high school after ten-plus years of experience in Family Meetings.

9. Use courtesy during the Meetings.

There are certain basic courtesies that you and your family should observe at every Meeting.

One person speaks at a time. In order to speak, you must be recognized by the Moderator. The Moderator's job is to see that everyone gets a turn to talk about the subject at hand.

There are no interruptions. Each person is allowed to express her thoughts fully even if no one else agrees with her. Everyone will get a turn. So there's no need to interrupt the present speaker or the Moderator.

There are no put-downs. Siblings have a tendency to demean or criticize one another's ideas. And parents can imply that a child's suggestions aren't any good. These responses are contrary to the basic spirit of your Family Meeting.

Family Meetings are confidential. This means that what you talk about during Meetings stays within the family. This allows individuals to talk freely about their thoughts and feelings. They don't have to fear their remarks will be broadcast or brought up to them later. Financial matters, personal problems, and negotiated agreements are particularly sensitive. Without everyone agreeing to strict confidentiality, Family Meetings can't develop the level of trust necessary to deal adequately with problems.

10. Make decisions by consensus, not voting.

How do you reach consensus? When it's time to choose a particular course of action, propose a solution. See if everyone can agree to it, or at least to try it. If any person doesn't agree, vary the solution until you can come to a mutually agreeable plan. Sometimes, for lack of time or agreement, a problem has to be tabled until the next Meeting.

Consensus decision-making means that parents can never be outvoted. If there is a proposed solution you can't agree to, don't. The group has to keep working on creating other solutions or refining the current one. It also means that children must agree to the proposal. Their feelings and ideas become an important part of the decision-making process. As you can see, this method requires a positive attitude toward problem-solving, negotiation, and compromise on everyone's part. This feature becomes more important in later parenting years.

11. Keep a Family Meeting log.

Write down your group decisions or plans for future reference. Often you may try a solution and later evaluate it. The log will prove very helpful in documenting exactly what was decided and when.

Also, family members can refer to it if they feel decisions are not being acted on, or if others are not living up to their agreements.

12. **Provide a treat.**

At the end of each Family Meeting you should have a snack or fun activity. This is a reward for the family's "hard work" and cooperation. The treat will depend on what time of day you have your Meeting. For example, if you hold it after dinner, you might provide dessert. A mid-afternoon Meeting treat could be a game or a family outing. And having your Meeting right before a meal will dictate yet another plan.

The treat need not be big, fancy, or expensive. It can be as simple as a stick of gum, a cookie, reading a story, or playing a favorite game. But it should be something your family members like so it will encourage them through the Meeting. After a while, you may find that the fellowship time while eating snacks or playing together is very valuable apart from the Meeting itself. If so, choose a treat that reinforces your family's sense of community and pleasure in one another.

13. **Follow through on whatever your family decides in the Meetings.**

You can't build positive family relationships by undermining or ignoring decisions you've made together. Abide by them in your daily life. If you didn't think you could, you should have voiced your concerns at the Meeting when they were discussed and agreed upon. If you do find difficulties in living out the decisions, bring them up at the next Family Meeting. Encourage your children to do the same.

Some men are reluctant to try Family Meetings. They fear it means giving up power or authority. Actually, this is far from the case. You gain *more* parental power and authority through the Meetings. Because you're treating your child as an individual whose ideas are worth listening to, he is less likely to behave in self-defeating and family-disrupting ways. He knows there is a forum where he can take any grievances. When he agrees to a solution, he is more likely to follow it. And he will be more inclined to develop a strong relationship with you because you have provided an atmosphere of trust and respect.

14. **Discuss ongoing concerns at regular intervals.**

Some major topics will reoccur throughout your parenting years. For example, managing a household is really an entire family's responsibility. So you frequently will need to address household chores as a specific agenda item.

One reason for this is that your child's contribution to chores depends on his age and development. An infant can't do any. A toddler can assist you in picking up his toys. However, a preschooler, especially an older one, can be helpful in many ways. His attention span is still relatively short, so he can't manage long or complex tasks. But a four- or five-year-old can sweep, bag leaves, help wash the car, fold and hang towels, assist in cooking, put his toys away, help sort the laundry, dust non-fragile items, set or clear the table, and so on.

Preschoolers like to do "real" work, especially with a parent. Your happy acceptance of this fact and your patient teaching of basic skills will provide the foundation for future participation at a higher level. Remember your goal to help your child grow into an independent and self-sufficient adult? To attain these characteristics he will need the skills to operate a household by himself. Learning these skills begins in the early years when he is eager to help.

As your child gets older, he may resist doing his share of the work. Family chores can become a volatile topic that needs regular attention. Here's an example of how the recurring issue of who does what chores can be resolved at Family Meetings.

Write down every job it takes to operate your home. List tasks in equal weights. For instance, "meal preparation" is not equivalent to "vacuuming the living room." After all, preparing a meal could include: plan the menus, shop, put the groceries away, cook, set the table, clear the table, put leftovers away, clean the table and counters, wash dishes, scrub pots and pans, etc. Doing these activities daily isn't equal in time or energy to vacuuming the living room once or twice a week. Try separating major chores into their various parts. This process may seem particularly detailed. But you only have to make the basic list once. As your family's needs grow, you can simply add other responsibilities to it. You won't have to rewrite it each time you reallocate household chores. Where appropriate, next to each chore put the day or time of day by which a chore must be completed.

The next step is for family members to alternate choosing chores from the list until every task is taken.

Be sure your child's selections are at a level that he can handle safely and will make him feel good about his contributions. For instance, he can jointly choose "grocery shopping" with you and provide real assistance. However, because of transportation and payment issues, he couldn't do the job alone. As he grows, he will be able to assume responsibility for completing entire chores by himself.

At the end of the list, there may be a few jobs no one wants to pick (such as "take out the trash" or "clean the bathroom"). You could agree to alternate these chores so that no one gets stuck with the most undesirable ones all of the time.

Family members perform their chosen chores for the next six months (or any other mutually agreed upon period). Then at a future Family Meeting, take out the list and choose again. Encourage everyone to try different tasks this time in order to expand their skills. If anyone needs help in learning how to do a certain chore, you can teach each other. In this way, all family members grow in experience and self-confidence. It also enables you to get beyond stereotypes.

••••

You will find that regular Family Tune-ups, in the form of Family Meetings, help you tackle problems while they're still small. This, in turn, creates a happier family life and more loving relationships—which is your ultimate goal.

THE WAY AHEAD

The fathering road is not always going to be smooth and level. You may not enjoy every part of the journey. There will be a mix of excitement and boredom, wonderful times and frustrations. That is reality. But what is most important through it all is to keep your outlook clear. Your wife and child need a warm, affectionate relationship with you—regardless of the circumstances. And, in order to really be a father, you need to experience that kind of relationship as well. This is what it means to enjoy full ownership of your fatherhood.

Again, **Good Luck and Happy Fathering**—now as well as down the road.

WARRANTY STATEMENT

This Warranty is good for up to FIVE YEARS of your fatherhood's relationships with no mileage limitations. To extend your warranty with the Manufacturer for another five years, you must obtain the book, **Fatherhood: An Owner's Manual, For Fathers of Children Aged 5 - 10.**

SECTION VI

APPENDICES

Here are additional resources to help you get the most out of your fatherhood:

A. Troubleshooting Guide
B. Thumbnail Sketch Of Child Development
C. How To Select Good Childcare
D. Reference Book List
E. Children's Literature List

APPENDIX A

Troubleshooting Guide

IF YOU ...	THEN ...
Want more time with your child	Do Parental Tune-up.
Want to find a hobby that fits your new family lifestyle	Check Priorities Cylinder. Ask Father Support Network. Do Personal Tune-up, Family Tune-up.
Feel mornings are too chaotic	Do Marital Tune-up, Family Tune-up.
Need more physical exercise	Check Priorities Cylinder. Do Personal Tune-up, Family Tune-up.
Feel like you don't have time to do anything important or interesting	Check Priorities Cylinder.
Are unsure about your benefits at work	Ask Father Support Network, and talk to your employer's Personnel Department.
Want to find good books to read to your child	Ask Father Support Network. Check Children's Literature List in Appendix E.
Need more help on positive discipline techniques	Check Reference Book List in Appendix D. Ask Father Support Network. Do Parental Tune-up.
Want to know more about preschools	Ask Father Support Network. Check How To Select Good Childcare in Appendix C, and Reference Book List in Appendix D.
Have trouble deciding what stage of growth your child is in	Read Gesell, Ilg, & Ames, *Infant And Child In The Culture Of Today, Rev. Ed.* Do Parental Tune-up. Ask child's pediatrician or childcare director.
Would like to take a parenting class but don't know where to find a good one	Ask Father Support Network. Check local community college, adult school, hospital, childcare referral agency, or parental stress group.
Feel more irritable lately	Check Brakes. Do Personal Tune-up.
Have new financial problems	Do Financial Tune-up.
Are upset by your wife's lack of interest in sex	Check Steering. Do Marital Tune-up.

Troubleshooting Guide

IF YOU ...	THEN ...
Are feeling lonely	Check Priorities Cylinder. Ask Father Support Network. Do Personal Tune-up, Marital Tune-up.
Expected more from your parenting experience	Ask Father Support Network. Do Marital Tune-up.
Thought fathering would be easier	Ask Father Support Network. Do Marital Tune-up, Parental Tune-up, Family Tune-up.
Feel jealous of your wife's time with the baby	Do Marital Tune-up, Parental Tune-up.
Want to parent differently than your dad did	Check all Cylinders, Spark Plug, and Fuel quality. Do Parental Tune-up. Ask Father Support Network.
Disagree with the way your wife handles the child	Check Steering. Do Parental Tune-up, Marital Tune-up.
Want to know more about your child's temperament	Do Parental Tune-up. Check Reference Book List in Appendix D.
Are having trouble dealing with the "terrible twos" stage	Check child growth and development, and discipline sections of Reference Book List in Appendix D. Do Parental Tune-up.
Sometimes feel overwhelmed by what it takes to be a good father	Check downshifting methods. Ask Father Support Network. Do Personal Tune-up, Marital Tune-up, Parental Tune-up, Family Tune-up.
Feel more impatient, frustrated, and/or angry at times	Check Priorities and Personal Growth Cylinders. Check Brakes, Steering, Spark Plug, and Fuel (use only what Manufacturer recommends). Do Personal Tune-up, Marital Tune-up, Parental Tune-up.
Want to know how to handle sibling rivalry better	Check discipline and communication sections of Reference Book List in Appendix D. Check Brakes and downshifting methods. Do Parental Tune-up, Family Tune-up.
Often seem bogged down in the day-to-day problems of parenting	Check Road Maps, macro-parenting. Ask Father Support Network. Do Parental Tune-up.

APPENDIX B

Thumbnail Sketch Of Child Development

As beginning parents, our knowledge of child development is both limited and general. Most of us realize that infants start out unable to do much. They steadily grow, and at five or six years enter school. And we know that teething, walking, talking, self-feeding, and toilet training occur sometime during these years. But we don't have a clear picture of how our children mature.

Emotional Development

We learn to marvel at our children's rapid physical and intellectual growth and skill development—from rolling over to running, and babbling to talking. What we often have difficulty understanding and dealing with is their *emotional* growth. We may feel shock or dismay when our children whine, have tantrums, reject us or our authority, say "No!" to reasonable requests, run the opposite way when we call them, cry uncontrollably for unknown reasons, suddenly start to cling like ivy, and the like. And these parental feelings bother us, because we thought that with loving care, "Our kids would never do that!"

Everyone's heard of the "terrible twos." This describes a particularly trying time in the emotional lives of children. They seem to take great pleasure in rebelling against their parents or caregivers. They are irritable, tempestuous, and generally out of sorts with the world. It's so predictable, you can anticipate it and even prepare for it.

But in actuality, there is "terrible twos" type behavior at each age and stage. Think of it this way. As your child gets older, he grows out of his clothing. He continually needs bigger sizes and different styles which better fit his changing physical abilities. There is a similar pattern to his emotional development. As he grows older, he needs to progress to new levels of maturity. In this case, his emotional "clothes"—his usual ways of relating—are too tight and restricting. So he must burst out of these old ways in order to move to a new skill level. And this is unsettling to him. It creates an emotional upheaval.

Your child has spent time at his present level of development, so he's used to it. He knows what he can handle. He's comfortable with himself. His experience fosters competence and confidence. However, when his built-in impetus toward growth drives him to the next level, suddenly everything seems strange. He must try out new skills, but he's clumsy at first. His sense of competence and his self-confidence drop. His frustrations, fears, and anxieties increase. And these are expressed in withdrawals, increased crying, emotional outbursts, and difficulties in all of his relationships.

After he gains some experience at his new stage of development, his behavior tends to even out. He's more socially and emotionally adept. He feels better about himself and his abilities. He enjoys a period of stability. But then, his inner growth needs drive him toward the next level of emotional and physical maturity. And the cycle repeats.

Simply put, your child will move constantly from stability to instability, and then forward to a time of stability again. This process is necessary and normal.

It's also a good sign because it means he is growing up. As his father, this is what you want. Through times of transition, you may frequently need to remind yourself: "Growing up is good. Periods of emotional instability in my child's life are part of growing up. In fact, they mean that he is normal. If my child never experienced these, he would remain an emotional infant forever. And I don't want that."

Stages of Growth

NOTE: Each child is an individual with his or her personal developmental timetable. However, all healthy children grow in a similar, sequential pattern. The following is a brief description of what is considered typical at a given age. This information is intended to give some perspective on the *flow* of child development. Allowing for differences means that your child can be somewhat ahead of or behind these stages and still be considered in the "normal" range of development. For in-depth information about all phases of child development, consult the book, *Infant And Child In The Culture Of Today, Revised Edition*, by Gesell, Ilg, and Ames; or the series *Your One Year Old* (*Two*, *Three*, etc.), by Ames and Ilg. One of these resources is a must for your reference shelf.

Birth. Your infant is born with the immediate need to master vital skills—breathing, sucking, digesting, seeing, and adjusting to new noises and temperatures. This is the ultimate time of transition from a stable situation to a new level of maturity.

One to Seven Months. Your child has adjusted to the initial birth experience. She's well on her way to learning a variety of activities—smiling, laughing, looking at people, responding to words and touch, grasping objects, and sleeping for longer periods of time.

Eight to Nine Months. During this stage, you may notice a time of physical transition and emotional instability. Your baby is strongly motivated to crawl. But he's not quite able to carry it off, which is a source of frustration. He becomes more wary of strangers as he begins to distinguish differences in people. Crying and laughter may be close together.

Ten to Fourteen Months. Your child becomes better adjusted to her new level. She responds to more variation in body language—gestures, sounds, facial expressions, touch. She's able to sit alone for longer periods of time, handle objects, get to her hands and knees, crawl, pull up to standing, start to walk, and enjoy social games, among other skills.

Fifteen Months to Two Years. You will begin to see significant changes during the next nine months. Now that she's more mobile, your child will continually explore. She'll walk, climb, fling, dart, and dash. She begins to express herself verbally. You will find her moods shifting. She may exhibit a temper, but it will be short-lived. Your "No-Nos" may have little effect.

From about 18 to 23 months, you will notice a small rebellious phase. Your child won't come when you call him. In fact, he may walk the other way when you approach. With his new-found mobility, he doesn't want to be limited by you or anything else. His frustration level is low, resulting in a quicker temper. He can't really share yet, which may cause trouble with siblings or friends.

Two Years. This is a time of emotional stability. She has incorporated her new level of language and physical skills. So she feels more comfortable and competent. She is more responsive and loving toward you. She is more apt to want to please you. And her frustration level is higher so she can wait longer for what she wants.

Two-and-a-Half Years. This is the well-known "terrible twos" stage. Be prepared. It is a time of transition and instability in all areas—social, cognitive, physical, and emotional. Your "angel" has turned sour. You won't believe it's the same child. You will doubt your parenting abilities.

He will be Mr. "No!", demanding, inflexible, domineering, and easily frustrated. Temper tantrums abound. He will quickly go from one emotional extreme to another. In short, he will not be easy to live with or handle. This is not a good time to demand consistent toilet training from him. Looking on the bright side, he will be vigorous, energetic, and enthusiastic.

Three Years. This is a period of stability for both you and your child. Your "angel" has returned, only older and better. She is now more social, can share more easily, begins to take turns, relates comfortably to others, has greater physical abilities, and is able to communicate more effectively. Because all these ingredients are at hand, this is a better time to begin total self-toileting or start preschool.

Three-and-a-Half Years. Don't get too relaxed. This is another stage of transition, similar to the "terrible twos." You will find your child exhibiting uncertainty, insecurity, greater anxiety, and a lack of coordination. He will have more difficulties in his relationships, language, and possibly with his vision and hearing.

Four Years. In a way, this is an extension of the three-and-a-half stage, only more sophisticated. Many people have described children at this stage as "out-of-bounds." Your child is more apt to hit, kick, or throw objects. Loud laughter can quickly alternate with rage. You may start hearing profanity (Where did she learn that!). She will disobey your requests and try to do things *her* way. This age is also one of great imagination, boasting, and tall tales. The line between truth and fiction is thin.

Four-and-a-Half Years. Your child may still be finishing the previous transition, but you will find this age to be an improvement. He will gain better control of his body. He is more adept at relationships. He enjoys discussing things with you at length. His frustration level is much higher. And he can begin many more activities by himself.

Five Years. Breathe a sigh of relief at this period of stability. You and your child have made it through the first five years. Overall, your child is doing well. She is becoming secure, capable, and well-adjusted in all areas of her life. She wants to behave and she has the capacity to do so. It's a delightful stage. It's a wonderful life, especially after living through the previous five-year developmental roller coaster ride.

APPENDIX C

How To Select Good Childcare

The first decision is whether or not to place your child in care. There are many pros and cons. Your choice may be shaped by the reality of family finances. But there are other important considerations, such as both parents' career goals, leave benefits, the health of family members including the baby, your child's developmental needs, the availability and expense of safe care, your parenting philosophy, and so on. Your family's needs and resources are unique. You and your wife should thoroughly discuss your options before coming to a joint decision.

If you decide to use it, good childcare is not something you can select in a hurry. It's very important that you put time and effort into the project. Start as early as you can. After all, what's involved is your child's health, safety, and happiness. You will want to find the best situation available.

Here is a list of questions to use in selecting a caregiver. These are only intended to help you get started. You will want to add your own specific concerns. For further information, check with your County Department of Social Services (or its equivalent), or a local Childcare Referral Agency.

Site

1. Is the childcare facility licensed? Although a license doesn't always mean high quality, it should be your minimum requirement for center-based care. Your state may not require licensing of small daycare homes for six or fewer children. Check local requirements with your County Childcare Referral Agency.

2. What do the facilities look like? Is there enough room? A well-lighted, cheerful environment? Is there a quiet, supervised sleeping area? Sufficient age-appropriate play equipment and toys? Are there options for active play indoors as well as outside? Are play surfaces and furnishings safe (for instance, tables with rounded

corners and washable surfaces, electrical outlets capped, or padding under climbing equipment)? Is everything reasonably clean and in good repair? Is it comfortably heated or air conditioned? Is there a fenced yard? Childproof latches on doors? Examine *every* room in the center, as well as the yard.

3. Are the meals or snacks nutritious and appetizing? How are allergies handled? Do parents provide their own child's food? Can fathers or nursing mothers come to feed their babies? Is the food preparation area clean?

4. Is emergency equipment available (smoke detectors, fire extinguishers, first aid supplies)? Are emergency procedures posted? Is there an evacuation plan? Are there clearly marked, multiple exits and fire escapes? Does it appear that all safety and building codes are being met?

5. Is there a supervised isolation area for children who become ill during care?

6. Are diapering areas located near sinks (away from food preparation) and equipped for proper sanitation procedures?

7. Is parking convenient and safe?

Staff

1. What are the qualifications of all staff members? Were their backgrounds checked with a law enforcement agency before employment? Were they required to have a physical exam and TB screening? Ask to meet and talk with those who would care for your child. What are your impressions? Is each person warm? Knowledgeable? Friendly?

2. Is parent-staff communication encouraged? Can you hold regular conferences? Do you receive daily feedback on your child's experiences in care? What is the procedure for handling a complaint?

3. What is the ratio of children to staff? Four to one is recommended for infants to toddlers, six to one for two-year-olds, and eight to one for three- to five-year-olds.

4. Meet and talk with the director of the facility. Is he or she the owner? If not, who is? Does the director have caregiving duties that will limit supervision of the other workers? What impressions do you have about this person and his or her leadership style and philosophy? Trust your intuition. If you feel negative or doubtful, do not use this caregiver.

5. How long have the most senior two or three staffers worked there? How long do most workers stay? Staff turnover rates may tell you something about the facility and its management. Frequent changes are not good for your child, who will then constantly need to adjust to new people and expectations.

6. How do caregivers handle discipline? Separation anxiety? Biting or other physically aggressive behavior?

7. Do teachers understand child growth and development? Do teachers have training in early childhood education?

8. Does the center encourage fathers to be actively involved in the lives of their children and even in the center? If not, move on.

Program

1. What is the daily schedule? Is there any flexibility in it? How are individual eating and sleeping needs handled? Is there a balance between child-initiated and group activities?

2. Are there indoor *and* outdoor play opportunities every day?

3. Are there both small-muscle activities (art, puzzles, construction and nesting toys, matching games, etc.) *and* large-muscle play equipment (balls, swings, climbing and balancing equipment, jumping tubes, riding toys, etc.)?

4. Are there different interest areas (housekeeping and dramatic play, books, puzzles and games, art, blocks, sand box or water play, etc.)?

5. What programs assist the child's social, emotional, and spiritual development? What values are being taught?

6. Are the center's activities non-sexist and non-racist? Look at the toys, books, music, and pictures, as well as the diversity of staff and their attitudes or comments. Do they have and teach stereotypes

about fathers and mothers, and how each "should" relate to work and children?

7. Do the children look relatively happy in the program?

8. Are particular holidays or religious events celebrated? Are these consistent with your beliefs? How do they handle birthdays?

9. Is TV or video watching a part of the program? If so, find out what is shown, how often, and how the content is extended through interactive play between the children and caregivers. Solid research shows that both the amount of TV viewing as well as inappropriate content can negatively affect your child's social, physical, and intellectual development.

10. What effort does the childcare provider make to keep parents informed about the program (activity schedules, newsletters, meetings, etc.)?

Policies, Fees, and Schedules

1. What are the policies of the center or provider? Ask for a written copy. Are they reasonable? Is there an emphasis on safety and health? Can you make unannounced drop-in visits? If the answer to the last question is "No," drop this childcare provider from consideration.

2. Will they provide a list of present and past parents as references?

3. Is parent participation required? Encouraged? Is there a fine for non-participation?

4. What are the illness policies? How does the center or provider prevent injuries or control the spread of infections?

5. Will the staff administer prescribed medicine for a non-communicable illness?

6. Is smoking allowed around the children or in rooms they will use? If so, drop this provider from consideration. Second-hand smoke is a proven health risk for your child.

7. What are the fees (or other payments) and when are they due? Is there a separate registration fee? Are there penalty fees (for instance, for late pick-ups)? How often do fees change?

8. Can your child's care schedule be changed to add or decrease days or hours?

9. Are there vacation or holiday periods when no care is offered?

10. Do you pay for care during extended absences (vacations, long illnesses, etc.)?

Follow-Up

After choosing and enrolling your child in care, be sure to stay active:

1. Get involved. Attend parent information meetings. Take time to participate in the program. Give encouraging, positive feedback to the staff.

2. Make drop-in visits. Use this time to quietly observe center routines and staff-child relationships. Do not monopolize staff attention.

3. Look for ways you can help your caregiver understand your child. Communicate regularly with the staff. Frequent short conversations while your child is still adapting may be helpful in the beginning. Quarterly conferences could be arranged thereafter. Provide information about family changes that might affect your child's behavior. Your sincere interest in your child's welfare and the success of the center's program will build a solid foundation for these occasions.

4. Make backup childcare plans in advance for when your child is sick, the center is closed, etc. Having two or more options available to you is preferable. Check with your local Childcare Referral Agency for resources in your community.

APPENDIX D

Reference Book List

Child Growth And Development

Don't Push Your Preschooler (Revised Ed.), by Louise Ames and Joan Chase (Harper & Row, 1980). Good reasons for a relaxed, developmentally aware parenting style during the first five years.

Infant And Child In The Culture Of Today (Revised Ed.), by Arnold Gesell, Frances Ilg, and Louise Ames (Harper & Row, 1974). Details child growth and development through the first five years. Excellent reference book; a must for every parent.

Know Your Child, by Stella Chess and Alexander Thomas (Basic, 1989). Good for understanding your child at all ages, even through the teen years. Discusses temperament.

Miseducation: Preschoolers At Risk, by David Elkind (Knopf, 1987). Describes what education is best for preschoolers.

The Plug-in Drug: Television, Children, & The Family, by Marie Winn (Viking Penguin, 1985). Shows the negative impact TV can have on children.

Unplugging The Plug-in Drug, by Marie Winn (Viking Penguin, 1987). Getting your children to turn off the TV.

Your One Year Old, by Louise Ames and Frances Ilg (Delacorte, 1983). Details characteristics and abilities of a one year old, including suggestions for parenting this age child. Part of a series—*Your Two Year Old*, *Your Three Year Old*, etc.

Communication

How To Talk So Kids Will Listen & Listen So Kids Will Talk, by Adele Faber and Elaine Mazlish (Avon, 1982). The title says it all. Good communication tools.

Predictive Parenting: What to Say When You Talk to Your Kids, by Shad Helmstetter (Pocket Books, 1990). Helps you evaluate what you say so you can get your message across better.

Talk With Your Child, by Harvey Wiener (Viking, 1988). Discusses how to develop your child's language and reading skills.

The Secret Language of Your Child, by David Lewis (St. Martin's Press, 1978). Parent-child communication from baby talk to body language. Good for understanding toddlers and preschoolers.

Discipline

Children: The Challenge, by Rudolph Dreikurs and Vicki Stolz (Dutton, 1987). Excellent book on understanding and handling children's misbehavior. Another must for your shelf.

How To Discipline With Love From Crib To College, by Fitzhugh Dodson (Signet, 1987). The title says it all.

How To Influence Children, by Charles Schaefer (Van Nostrand Reinhold, 1978). Gives many positive parenting options to handle misbehavior.

Love and Discipline, by Barbara Brenner (Ballantine, 1988). Excellent suggestions on how to set and keep limits.

Parenting Young Children, by Don Dinkmeyer, Sr., Gary McKay, and James Dinkmeyer (American Guidance, 1989). Intended as a course book for S.T.E.P. classes; a good resource for positive methods of relating to young children.

The Preschool Years, by Ellen Galinsky and Judy David (Random, 1988). Deals with constructive strategies for living with children ages two to five.

To Listen to a Child, by T. Berry Brazelton (Addison-Wesley, 1986). Guidelines for helping children deal with basic experiences from fear to thumbsucking.

Without Spanking or Spoiling, A Practical Approach to Toddler and Preschool Guidance, by Elizabeth Crary (Parenting Press, 1992). Shows that there are many constructive ways to teach children how to behave without using spanking.

Family Life

On Becoming A Family, by T. Berry Brazelton (Delacorte, 1981). Excellent description of growing family relationships from pregnancy through very early parenting.

Secrets Of Strong Families, by Nick Stinette and John Defrain (Berkley Books, 1985). The results of research on strong families. Food for thought.

Siblings Without Rivalry, by Adele Faber and Elaine Mazlish (Avon, 1988). Excellent book if you also have another child.

The Stressless Home, by Robert and Susan Bramson (Ballantine, 1987). Strategies for home and family organization to reduce everyone's stress.

The Winning Family: Increasing Self-Esteem In Your Children And Yourself (Revised Ed.), by Louise Hart (Lifeskills Press, 1990). Insights on helping your child develop this important trait.

Tips For Working Parents, by Kathleen McBride (Storey Communications Inc., 1989). Time, career, and family management ideas.

Family Meetings

A Family Meeting Handbook: Achieving Family Harmony Happily, by Robert Slagle (Family Relations, 1987). Helpful guidance on establishing Family Meetings.

Raising Kids Who Can: Using Family Meetings to Nurture Responsible, Cooperative, Caring, and Happy Children, by Betty Bettner and Amy Lew (Harper Perennial, 1992). The title says it all.

Fathering

Between Father and Child, by Ronald Levant and John Kelly (Viking, 1989). Helps men improve their communication and relationship skills. Gives examples with older children, but now's the time to start.

Father and Child, by Robert Osterman, Christopher Spurrell, and Carolyn Chubet (Longmeadow, 1991). Covers tips for the period of pregnancy through the child's second year.

Fatherhood In America: A History, by Robert Griswold (Basic Books, 1993). For you history buffs—fatherhood since 1800.

Fathers And Families: Paternal Factors In Child Development, by Henry Biller (Auburn House, 1993). Shows the tremendous importance of a father in the life of his child. Supported by decades of research. Another must book.

Finding Our Fathers: The Unfinished Business of Manhood, by Samuel Osherman (The Free Press, 1986). Gives insights on how your relationship with your father (or lack of one) affects your current life.

Finding Time For Fathering, by Mitch and Susan Golant (Fawcett Columbine, 1992). Describes the importance of fathering today, and how fathers can become constructively involved.

How To Father A Sucessful Daughter, by Nicky Marone (Fawcett Crest, 1988). Helpful advice on how fathers can help daughters grow through the years to become happy, confident women.

Man Enough: Fathers, Sons, and the Search for Masculinity, by Frank Pittman (G.P. Putnam's Sons, 1993). A thoughtful discussion on how to be masculine and a loving father today.

Pregnant Fathers, by Jack Heinowitz (Prentice Hall, 1982). Discusses issues of interest to pregnant fathers.

The Father's Almanac (Revised Ed.), by S. Adams Sullivan (Doubleday, 1992). Filled with ideas for fun father-child activities.

The Nurturing Father, by Kyle Pruett (Warner Books, 1987). Details a nurturing father's positive impact on children.

Kids And Books

Choosing Books For Kids, by Joanne Oppenheim, Barbara Brenner, and Betty Boegehold (Ballantine, 1986). How to choose age-appropriate books. (For additional recommended children's books, see Appendix E, Children's Literature List.)

Give Your Child A Head Start In Reading, by Fitzhugh Dodson (Fireside, 1981). Tells you how to do it.

Medical Reference Books

Dr. Spock's Baby and Child Care, by Benjamin Spock and Michael Rothenberg (Dutton, 1992). Make sure you get the most current edition. Excellent on medical questions.

American Red Cross First Aid and Safety Handbook, by the American Red Cross staff and Kathleen Handal (Little, 1992). Another must book for your family.

APPENDIX E

Children's Literature List

Here is a basic list of children's picture books and easy readers in which fathers are depicted as competent, sensitive, or involved parents and important in the lives of their children. These are books you will not be ashamed to read with your child. Look for them in your library or bookstore. If you have other "nominees" for this list, please contact the Publisher. They may appear in future revised editions.

Excellent

Bailey, Debbie, *My Dad* (Annick Press)

Banish, Roslyn, *I Want To Tell You Something About My Baby* (Wingbow Press)

Baum, Louis, *One More Time* (Mulberry Books)

Bernstein, J. and Fireside, B., *Special Parents, Special Children* (Albert Whitman)

Blaine, M., *The Terrible Thing That Happened At Our House* (Four Winds Press)

Bradman, Tony, *The Sandal* (Viking Kestrel)

Brown, Myra Berry, *Somebody's Pup* (Macmillan)

Bunting, Eve, *The Wall* (Clarion)

Diot, Alain, *Better, Best, Bestest* (Harlin Quist)

Dragonwagon, Crescent, *Wind Rose* (Harper & Row)

Etherington, Frank, *When I Grow Up Bigger Than Five* (Annick Press)

Grindley, Sally, *Knock, Knock! Who's There?* (Knopf/Dragonfly)

Hamilton, Morse, *Who's Afraid Of The Dark?* (Avon/Camelot)

Hines, Anna Grossnickle, *Daddy Makes The Best Spaghetti* (Clarion Books)

Ketteman, Helen, *Not Yet, Yvette* (Albert Whitman)

Lewis, Thomas P., *Frida's Office Day* (Harper & Row)

Littledale, Harold, *Alexander* (Parents)

Mandelbaum, Pili, *You Be Me, I'll Be You* (Kane/Miller)

McPhail, David, *Emma's Pet* (Dutton/Unicorn)

McPhail, David, *Farm Morning* (Harcourt/Voyager)

McPhail, David, *The Party* (Little, Brown & Co.)

Merriam, Eve, *Daddies At Work* (Simon Schuster)

O'Brien, Anne Sibley, *It's Hard To Wait* (Henry Holt)

Porte, Barbara Ann, *Harry's Mom* (Dell)

Porte, Barbara Ann, *Harry's Dog* (Scholastic)

Porter-Gaylord, Laurel, *I Love My Daddy Because ...* (Dutton)

Rabin, Berniece, *Where's Chimpy?* (Albert Whitman)

Rogers, Fred, *Going To The Hospital* (Putnam)

Rogers, Fred, *Going To The Potty* (Putnam)

Rogers, Fred, *When A Pet Dies* (Putnam)

Rosenbaum, Eileen, *Ronnie* (Parents)

Ross, Jan, *Dogs Have Paws* (Modern Curriculum Press)

Slier, Debby and Lipp, Jane, *Me And My Dad* (Checkerboard Press)

Thompson, Susan, *One More Thing, Dad* (Albert Whitman)

Wahl, Jan, *Humphrey's Bear* (Henry Holt)

Ziefert, Harriet, *Daddy, Can You Play With Me?* (Puffin)

Zola, Meguido, *Only The Best* (Julia MacRae Books)

Zolotow, Charlotte, *The Summer Night* (Harper & Row)

Good

Alda, Arlene, *Matthew And His Dad* (Little Simon)

Asch, Frank, *Goodnight Horsey* (Prentice-Hall)

Asch, Frank, *Sand Cake* (Parents)

Baker, Betty, *My Sister Says* (Macmillan)

Bang, Molly, *Ten, Nine, Eight* (Mulberry Books)

Blake, Robert, *The Perfect Spot* (Philomel Books)

Brown, Marc, *Arthur's Pet Business* (Little, Brown & Co.)

Bunting, Eve, *Ghost's Hour, Spook's Hour* (Clarion)

Butterworth, Nick, *My Dad Is Awesome* (Candlewick Press)

Caines, Jeannette, *Daddy* (Harper & Row)

Cameron, Ann, *The Stories Julian Tells* (Knopf/Bullseye)

Carrick, Carol, *Ben And The Porcupine* (Clarion)

Carrick, Carol, *The Accident* (Clarion)

Carrick, Carol, *The Foundling* (Clarion)

Chenery, Janet, *The Toad Hunt* (Harper & Row)

Claverie, Jean, *Working* (Crown)

Cole, Joanna, *Your New Potty* (Morrow Junior Books)

Crows, Robert L., *Clyde Monster* (Dutton/Unicorn)

Ehrlich, Amy, *Zeek Silver Moon* (Dial-Pied Piper)

Flourney, Valerie, *The Best Time Of Day* (Random/Please Read To Me)

Friend, Dave, *Baseball, Football, Daddy And Me* (Puffin)

George, Jean Craighead, *The Wentletrap Trap* (E.P. Dutton)

Girard, Linda Walvoord, *At Daddy's On Saturday* (Albert Whitman)

Greenfield, Eloise, *Daddy And I* (Black Butterfly Children's Books)

Greenfield, Eloise, *First Pink Light* (Scholastic)

Greenspun, Adele Aron, *Daddies* (Philomel Books)

Hamilton, Virginia, *Drysolong* (Harcourt Brace Jovanovich)

Haseley, Dennis, *Kite Flier* (Macmillan)

Haseley, Dennis, *My Father Doesn't Know About The Woods And Me* (Atheneum)

Hazen, Barbara Shook, *Tight Times* (Puffin)

Henkes, Kevin, *Bailey Goes Camping* (Puffin)

Hoban, Russell, *Nothing To Do* (Scholastic)

Horner, Althea J., *Little Big Girl* (Human Sciences Press)

Hutchins, Pat, *You'll Soon Grow Into Them, Titch* (Puffin)

Impey, Rose, *Desperate For A Dog* (Puffin)

Isadora, Rachel, *At The Crossroads* (Scholastic)

Kamen, Gloria, *Second-Hand Cat* (Atheneum)

Kidd, Nina, *June Mountain Secret* (HarperCollins)

Lewin, Hugh, *Jafta's Father* (Carolrhoda Books)

Long, Earlene, *Gone Fishing* (Houghton Mifflin)

Marzollo, Jean, *Amy Goes Fishing* (Dial Easy-To-Read)

Mayer, Mercer, *Just Go To Bed* (Golden)

Mayer, Mercer, *Just Me And My Dad* (Golden)

Ness, Evaline, *Sam, Bangs, & Moonshine* (Henry Holt, & Co.)

Oppenheim, Shulamith Levey, *The Lily Cupboard* (HarperCollins)

Ormerod, Jan, *Dad's Back* (Lothrop, Lee, & Shepard)

Ormerod, Jan, *Reading* (Lothrop, Lee, & Shepard)

Perrine, Mary, *Salt Boy* (Houghton Mifflin)

Rylant, Cynthia, *Henry And Mudge In Puddle Trouble* (Aladdin Books)

Rylant, Cynthia, *Henry And Mudge In The Sparkle Days* (Aladdin Books)

Schumacher, Claire, *A Big Chair For Little Bear* (Random/Please Read To Me)

Seeger, Pete, *Abiyoyo* (Macmillan)

Shavlev, Meir, *My Father Always Embarrasses Me* (Wellington Publishing)

Simon, Norma, *I'm Busy, Too* (Albert Whitman)

Turkle, Brinton, *Obadiah The Bold* (Viking)

Viorst, Judith, *The Tenth Good Thing About Barney* (Aladdin/Atheneum)

Watanabe, Shigeo, *Daddy, Play With Me!* (Philomel Books)

Watanabe, Shigeo, *I Can Take A Bath* (Philomel Books)

Watanabe, Shigeo, *Where's My Daddy?* (Philomel Books)

Watson, Jane Werner, et al, *Sometimes A Family Has To Move* (Crown Publishers)

Watson, Jane Werner, et al, *Sometimes I'm Afraid* (Golden Press)

Watson, Jane Werner, et al, *Sometimes I'm Jealous* (Golden Press)

Wells, Rosemary, *Shy Charles* (Puffin)

Yolen, Jane, *Owl Moon* (Scholastic)

INDEX

About The Author

Doug Spangler wrote a fathers' column in *American Baby* magazine for eight years. He also wrote a newspaper column, "Memo To Dads," and co-produced the local TV series, "Father Time." He has appeared on national TV to discuss fatherhood. Doug has been teaching parent education and fathering classes and workshops since 1980. He holds a seminary degree, a Master's degree in Counseling, and a teaching credential. He and his wife live in the San Francisco Bay Area. They are the parents of two young adult children.

This **Manual** makes a perfect gift for any new father in your life. Additional copies are available through your favorite bookstore, or you can order directly from the Publisher: